A REVIEW

OF THE

UNCONSTITUTIONAL LAWS,

OF THE

TWELFTH LEGISLATURE

OF TEXAS,

AND THE

OPPRESSIONS

OF THE

PRESENT ADMINISTRATIONS

EXPOSED,

—BY—

CHAS. B. PEARRE,

ATTORNEY AT LAW,

WACO, TEXAS.

J. D. LIPSCOMB & CO., PRINTERS,

61 Exchange Place, BALTIMORE, MD.

1872.

A REVIEW OF THE LAWS

OF THE

Twelfth Legislature

OF THE

STATE OF TEXAS,

Enacted in the Year 1870 and 1871,

AND THE

OPPRESSIONS

OF

GOVERNOR E. J. DAVIS' ADMINISTRATION

EXPOSED,

—BY—

CHARLES B. PEARRE,

ATTORNEY AT LAW,

WACO, TEXAS.

J. D. LIPSCOMB & CO., PRINTERS,

61 Exchange Place, BALTIMORE, MD.

TO

THE PEOPLE OF TEXAS.

FELLOW CITIZENS

I present you a short review of some of the obnoxious laws passed during the present administration of the government of Texas, and expose some of the frauds and oppressions of the party in power, and hope that this tyranny and misrule, ere long, may give place to simple justice and pure patriotism.

YOUR OBEDIENT SERVANT,

CHARLES B. PEARRE.

CHAPTER 1.

A Review of The Unconstitutional Laws passed by the Twelfth Legislature of The State of Texas.

We purpose under this head to write a Review of the administration of the government of Texas from the inauguration of Edward J. Davis as Governor, down to the adjournment of the Twelfth Legislature on the 2nd of December 1871.

We will first state the circunstances by which the people of Texas were surrounded at the time the present Constitution of the State was formed.

We were then governed as a military province of the United States, and the government of the state was placed in the hands of J. J. Reynolds, Colonel in the U. S. Army. An election was ordered by the military commander throughout the state for members to a State Convention, whose duty it should be to frame a Constitution for the State, after which the said Constitution was to be submitted to the people for ratification or rejection; and if ratified, it was then to be submitted to the Congress of the United States for acceptance before it became of any force or effect. At an election held in November 1869 the Constitution was ratified by a majority of the votes cast. The Constitution itself provided for the holding of an election at the same time and place for Senators and Representatives in the Legislature and for all State, District and County officers, who were to be elected by the people under the Constitution.

It is not our intention now to urge any objections to the Constitution, or to point out its defects; but simply to show *by whom* it was ordained and established, *for whom* it was ordained and established, *for what* it was ordained and established, *over whom* it was ordained and established. The preamble to the Constitution plainly shows *by whom* it was ordained,—"We the People of Texas *** do hereby ordain and establish this Constitution."

It is evident from hence that it was ordained and established by the people of Texas.

We will now show *for whom* it was ordained. It was ordained and established for *the People of Texas*. This is shown from the preamble; "We the people of Texas, acknowledging with gratitude the grace of God, in permitting us to make a choice of *our* form of government, do hereby ordain and establish this Constitution." *Our* form of government evidently means the form of government for "*we the People of Texas*."

We will have little difficulty in showing *for what* it was ordained and established. The preamble to the Bill of Rights designates the objects to be "that the heresies of nullification and secession, which brought the country to grief, may be eliminated from future political discussion; that public order may be restored, private property and human life protected; and the great principles of liberty and equality secured to us and our posterity." To effect these objects, to use the language of the framers, "we declare that," and they go on declaring the language of the Constitution. The Constitution was then ordained and established to secure to the people of Texas and their posterity the great principles of Liberty.

It was ordained and established for themselves.

We have yet to determine *over whom* this Constitution was ordained and established. It was *over* the government which *it* created, and *over all its officers* in their official character, and over every person inhabiting the State of Texas, to the full extent of the powers therein delegated, and no further. This Constitution was not the act of a government, but of the people organizing or constituting a government; and all government without a Constitution is power without a right.

All power exercised over a people must have some beginiung. It must be either delegated by the people, or it must be assumed by a self-constituted power. All delegated power is trust, and all assumed power is usurpation.

The conclusion is irresistible from what has been said, that the government which this Constitution creates can only exercise such powers as are therein delegated to it, and can only exercise those powers in the manner and for the purposes therein expressed. For instance, the Constitution gives the Governor the power to call forth the militia, to *execute the laws* of the State, to *suppress* insurrections, and *repel* invasions. If he calls them out for any other purpose, he becomes an usurper, or if he uses them for any other purpose after they are called out he violates his oath of office, and assumes to do that which he is prohibited from doing by the very power which created him and limits his power and defines the time when, and the manner in which he shall exercise it. The government or any branch of it may violate the provisions of the Constitution as effectually by exercising the powers therein delegated in a manner different from that therein prescribed, or for different purposes than those therein declared, as it may by assuming to itself the exercise of powers therein prohibited.

In pursuing this subject we intend to state only facts, and to draw such conclusions from them as necessarily force themselves upon the mind and convince the reason of all men who think for themselves.

The election which resulted in placing E. J. Davis in the Chief Executive office of the State took place at a time when a very large proportion of the most intelligent and best citizens of Texas was disfranchised by the laws then existing, and from this fact we are borne out in saying that E. J. Davis was not the choice of the people of Texas,

The facts also abundantly show that the returns from many counties, which gave Gen. Hamilton large majorities, were fraudulently and illegally thrown out; and for this reason E. J. Davis was not the choice of the people who were then entitled to vote, nor was he the choice of the people who actually did vote in the election for Governor.

The frauds and oppressions which were practiced during that election are still fresh in the minds of the people which renders it unnecessary here to recount them.

The facts we have stated concerning the election for Governor apply with equal if not greater force to the election for members of the Legislature, from which it follows naturally that a large number of men were returned who received a minority of the votes cast. We need not add that all such were Radicals.

This "so-called" Twelfth Legislature was brought together by corruption by intimidation by violent exertions of the military rule and by fraudulent distortions of law. It was therefore not to be expected that such an assembly was or ever could become a free and lawful Legislature. It was evidently impossible to obtain such under the circumstances; nor was it the wish or desire of those who controlledd and irected the election. The management of the whole affair was in the hands of the Radicals. Only such registrars, judges of elections, and other officers were appointed as would avail themselves of the slightest pretence to declare the Radical candidate duly elected. Every man from the highest to the lowest, who was placed in office then was made plainly to understand if he wished to retain his office he must at that juncture support the party candidate by his vote and interest—by foul as well as fair means.

It is no wonder under this state of facts that men asked each other, with no small anxiety, whether the votes would be fairly taken, counted and returned; and if those Democrats who received a majority of the votes would be *allowed* to take their seats.

The manner in which the election was conducted, and the disabilities resting upon so large a number of our best and most experienced citizens, satisfactorily account for the inexperience, lack of intelligence, and want of moral honesty in so unusually large a number of the members composing both branches of the Legislature.

When this body assembled in the city of Austin on the 26th day of April 1870, they excited in the minds of the people no expectation or even hope that their deliberations would result in any good to the State. And if our readers will follow us closely through this review of their acts we think they will be convinced that the people of Texas have not been disappointed in them.

The Governor in his proclamation of April 2nd 1870 convening the Legislature, requests the Senate and House of Representatives to come together and "inaugurate the regular State government, and to enter upon such general and special legislation as may be in *compliance* with the *spirit* and *letter* of the Constitution recently adopted by the people of Texas."

We shall see in our progress how he and the Legislature have carried out the letter of their proclamation in the acts which he has recommended, which it has passed, and he approved.

The Governor in his first message to the Legislature recommends "that a police system be adopted, embracing the whole State under one head," and says that no system of laws for the suppression of crime however severe will be complete "without such powers are conferred on the Executive as will enable him in any emergency to act with authority of law." He submits to the Legislature "the question of making some provision for the temporary establishment of martial law," and thinks that the mere knowledge of the fact that such power is given the Executive will go far to prevent the necessity of its execution.

The whole tenor of the Governor's first message to the Legislature evinces a craving and unnatural desire on his part to concentrate in himself all the powers of the government. He boldly and unblushingly recommends the Legislature to place such extraordinary powers in his hands as are in direct conflict with the letter and spirit of the Constitution of the State.

The sum and substance of his desire is, that the Legislature shall pass an act granting him the power to override the written Constitution of the State, unchecked to trample upon the liberties of the people, and to dispense with the statutes of the State in particular cases, and for special reasons known only to himself; and to deal with the liberty, property and character of the citizen in just such manner as his whims or prejudices may dictate. And in order that the grant of this power may be rendered available in his hands, he sees the necessity of organizing a strong military force in such manner and composed of such material as he may select. The Governor's Legislature in order to enable him effectually to put his iron heel upon the necks of the people and totally destroy their constitutional and legal rights, passed the act entitled "*An act to provide for the enrollment of the Militia, the organization and discipline of the State Guard and for the public defence.*"

In Section 1st they designate who shall be subject to military duty, "all able-bodied male *citizens residing* in the *State* between the ages of eighteen and forty-five years," excepting certain classes therein specified. By Section 2d the Governor is made commander-in-chief of all the military forces of the State. The forces are divided into two classes viz:—"the State Guard of Texas and the *Reserve* Militia."

Section 3d. "The State Guard of Texas shall consist of male

persons between the ages of eighteen and forty-five, who shall voluntarily enroll and uniform themselves for service therein; *provided* the Commander-in-Chief (the Governor) shall designate the number of men in each county in this State allowed to enroll in the State Guards, and have power to *reject any person* offering himself for enrollment in the same."

The Legislature in this section has enabled the Governor to organize an army unlimited in number, to be composed of such material as suits his inclination.

This army may be composed entirely of men unidentified with the interest or feelings of the people of Texas, and opposed to our political and religious liberty. In may be composed in whole or in part of foreigners imported for the purpose of swelling the ranks of this army.

If any honest good citizen who loves our religion and reveres the time honored principles of our free institutions should apply for enrollment in this army, the Governor may challenge him peremptorily, he must stand aside, and give place to such as better suit the aims and purposes of the Governor.

We desire to draw the attention of our readers to the very important fact that this act permits ablebodied male *citizens resident in the State* to enroll in the Reserve Militia, but all persons without qualification between the ages of eighteen and fortyfive years, can enroll in the State Guards, provided they suit the purposes of the Governor. Why this distinction? The common sense of every man will suggest to his mind the answer. This State Guard is peculiarly the Governor's Army, selected and organized out of such material as will serve his purposes. The Reserve Militia can only be composed of resident citizens of Texas, and perhaps would refuse to murder, rob and pilfer their fellow citizens should they be called upon so to do by the Commander-in-chief. They are what this Act designates them, "Reserve".

They cannot act unless called out by the Commander-in-chief. They remain unorganized, unarmed, and unequipped; but we find the State Guard fully organized and equipped, scattered through every or nearly every county in the State, eating up the substance of the people, and in very many instances murdering innocent and unoffending citizens—depriving them of their property by force or fraud, disturbing the peace and quiet of whole communities, and inflaming the animosities of the races; in a word, fully carrying out the purposes and interest of their organization. To use the governor's own language, the Legislature in the passage of this Act has conferred upon the Executive "*such powers as will enable him in any emergency to act with authority of law,*" if he consider this enactment authority of law. Undiscerning men would think that the posession of such unprecedented power would satisfy the cravings even of the Governor, but not so. He calls loudly for more *power*, and obtains it from his subservient Legislature. He calls upon them for power under certain contingencies (he to be the exclusive judge of the contingencies) to establish *martial law* in any section or sections of the State. The Legislature promptly responds to the desire of the Governor in the 26 Section of the Militia Bill, thus, "It shall be the duty of the Governor, and he is hereby authorized *whenever in his opinion* the enforcement of the law of this State is obstructed within any county or counties by combinations of lawless men too strong for the control of the civil authorities, to declare such county or counties under martial law, and to *suspend the laws therein* until the Legislature shall convene and take such action as it may deem necessary." This Section is in every part unconstitutional and violative of every principle of our Republican form of government, and altogether unnecessary to the full and perfect execution of the laws of the State. The Constitution vests in the Governor all the powers necessary, having a due regard to the protection of the liberties of the people. Article VI,

Section first, vests in the Governor the power "to call forth the Militia to execute the laws of the state, to suppress insurrection, and repel invasions." What more power does he need to enable him to carry out the legitimate functions of his office than is here given? It follows that the motive of the Governor in obtaining from the Legislature this extraordinary and unnecessary power was for other purposes than the execution of the laws of the State, the suppression of insurrection and the repelling of invasions. We see that the Constitution gave him abundant power to accomplish this. If the power to make laws or suspend them, rested with the governor, or become, under any state of facts necessary, to the proper discharge of the duties of his office, under our form of government, that power would be found in the written Constitution of the State. That it is not found there, proves that, no such power exists in the Government. Then what was his motive in securing to himself such power? I would that every citizen of Texas would demand from him an answer to this question. That universal shriek which comes up from the oppressed, downtrodden and outraged people of Texas tells plainly what his motive was. The malicious and wanton manner in which he has used this power declare in thunder tones what his motive was. The oppressed, robbed and slandered citizens of Limestone and Freestone counties both feel and say what his motive was. The people of Hill and other counties throughout the state, where he established his military commissioners and persecuted innocent citizens, with sad hearts and empty pockets can tell you what his motive was. The people of all those counties throughout the State who were prevented from reaping the benefits of their right of franchise, both by word and look, tell us what his motive was. If there are any who are yet skeptical as to the true motive of the Governor we refer them for light to the character and standing of the creatures he has enrolled in the

"*State Guard.*" They are a motley crowd, composed in part of foreigners unacquainted with the habits and character of our people, unidentified with us in interest or feeling, and in many instances unable to speak or even understand our language. Composed in part of gamblers, drunkards, fugitives from justice, escaped convicts, many of whom have the *mark* of Cain upon them; of such men as are capable of committing crimes of the darkest dye. The freedmen who are enrolled, with a very few exceptions, are such as are most vindictive against the white race, ignorant, lazy, and totally destitute of honesty. To be a moderate man in politics, to be a Conservative or Democrat, is such a disqualification as renders him unfit to be enrolled in the *State Guards.*

History speaks of no army which in every respect equals the Governor's army of *State Guards*, unless it be Tyrconnel's Irish army organized in the reign of James II, A. D. 1686. The motive in organizing this army can be better gathered from the language of the historian than from ours: "James," says Macauly "instead of allaying the animosities of the two populations inflamed it to a height before unknown. He determined to reverse their relative position, and to put the Protestant Calvinists under the feet of the Popish Celts. To be of the established religion, to be of the English blood, was in his veiw a disqualification for civil and military employment. Unhappily James instead of becoming a *mediator*, became the fiercest and *most reckless of partisans.*"

For these and other like outrages upon the liberties of the people of England James lost his crown and had to seek protection and a home in France. Yet it was the boast of *his* friends and partisans that during his reign the *writ* of *Habeas Corpus* was not once suspended. The friends and partisans of the oppressor of the people of Texas in that respect are not so fortunate as those of the tyrant James II.

It may perhaps, be asked, is not the Legislature more to blame for conferring these unnecessary and unconstitutional powers upon the Governor, than he is for accepting and exercising them? We unhesitatingly and truthfully answer, no! That Legislature at the date of the passage of the Militia Bill, was as completely under the control of Governor Davis as ever was a puppet in the hands of the wire-puller. In fact *he was the Legislature*, his word was law, his frown was terror, his smile joy. He is therefore wholly responsible for every offensive and unwarranted act passed. But this by no means relieves the members of the Legislature of the just odium of their acts, but only renders them more despicable in the eyes of just men. The act of which we have been speaking was approved by the Governor June 24th, 1870.

We now come to the Act of July 1st, 1870, entitled "*an act to establish a State Police, and provide for the regulation and government of the same.*" This wing of the Governor's army is to be composed of one Chief of Police, four Captains, eight Lieutenants, twenty Sargeants, and two hundred and twenty privates; the pay of privates to be sixty dollars, Sargeants seventy-five dollars, Lieutenants one hundred dollars, Captains one hundred and twenty-five dollars each, per month.

The Chief of this Police force is to be appointed by the Governor by and with the advice and consent of the Senate, and receives a salary of two thousand five hundred dollars per annum.

Sec. 3d empowers the Governor, or Chief of Police, with the approval of the Governor to remove at will any of the members of the State Police. Sec. 4 authorizes the Chief of Police, with the Governors's approval to make all rules and regulations for the government of the State Police. Sec. 5th enables the Governor to control, direct, and displace every executive officer in the State. How monstrous! how unconstitutional and how dangerous to the liberties of the people in this section! It would have disgraced the lawmakers of the Dark Ages, and we may rest assured that it will not fail to load the memory of the Governor and those Legislators who voted for it with the infamy which of right belongs to them. I will quote this Section in full; read it carefully and understandingly, and tell me what are your rights under this administration and what your liberties are worth?

Sec. 5th. "All sheriffs and their deputies, constables, marshals of cities and towns and their deputies and police of towns and cities, shall be considered as part of the State Police, and be subject to the supervisory control of the Governor and Chief of State Police, may, at any time be called upon to act in concert with the State Police in preventing or suppressing crime, or in bringing to justice offenders. The Chief of State Police, subject to approval of the Governor, may make all needful rules and regulations for the *government* and direction of these officers in matters looking to the maintenance of public peace, preventing or suppressing crime, and bringing to justice offenders; (mark what follows,) and *any* of these *officers* failing or refusing *prompt* obedience to such rules and regulations, or to the *orders* of the Governor or Chief of Police *shall be removed from office*," and suffer such other punishment as may be prescribed by law. We perceive from this section of the Act, that all the civil executive officers of the State are incorporated into and made a part of the State Police, and are subject to such rules and regulations as the Chief of Police with the Governor's approval may make for the direction of these executive peace officers; and if any of these officers of the Civil Government fail or refuse prompt obedience to these rules and regulations or to the *orders* of the Governor or Chief of State Police, shall be removed from office, not from the office, which he may hold by virtue of his connection with the State Police, but from his civil office of sheriff, constable, or marshal, as the case may be. These offices they hold or *ought to hold* by the suffrages of the people. The Constitution of the State declares in so many words that the sheriffs of the counties shall be elected by the qualified voters thereof. *Is* this section constitutional? We think no honest man who has ever read the Bill of Rights will hesitate for a second in pronouncing this section wickedly unconstitutional. To prove which, we need only quote Article I, Section seventeenth of the Bill of Rights. "The military shall at all times be subordinate to the civil authority."

We certainly live in a remarkably strange age. This is the first time in the experience of the world that any legislative body under any form of government whatsoever, in any country, civilized or uncivilized, christianized or barbarous, has passed a law giving to the very breath of the nostrils of the Chief Executive officer of the State the force and authority of law, with power to vacate every executive civil office in the State at his will and pleasure. The members who *knowingly* voted for this Bill, are traitors to their country, traitors to their children, traitors to their God who gave them life and liberty, and are not worthy to be called men. Compared with these Nero was a patriot worthy to be held in remembrance.

This is strange language but just, and justly merited.

We propose to show from the very letter and spirit of the Acts passed by this Twelfth Legislature that they have placed in the hands of the Governor the power to enable him at any time to completely upset, overturn and destroy the whole fabric and machinery of the civil government of the State, and erect upon its ruins a strange military despotism, maintained and supported by a standing army, unlimited in numbers. And we fear that there is much more probability of this being done, than many persons are disposed to imagine.

Such is the tendency of the policy of every Radical government in the South and (it may with truth be said,) in the North. The government of the United States, and the governments in nearly all of the several states have become centralized. High officers are looked to as embodying all the law, power and authority in the state. The officers do not look to the Constitution and the laws of the state for their authority to act, but to the officers who are higher in authority than themselves. Their commands are implicitly obeyed and carry with them the force and authority of law. The Radical Governors of the States, and particularly of the Southern States, look up to President Grant as the embodyment of all the laws, of all the Constitutions, and of all the powers, of all the governments, of all the states, in the United States.

Every observing man is forced to admit that the tendency all over the United States is towards centralization and despotism; and unless this tendency is soon checked the last vestige of our liberties will be swept away.

The shadows of these coming events may be seen even *now* by the diligent observer. It therefore behooves us to be vigilant and to be always awake and on our guard.

By the ninth section of this Act, the Governor is enabled to put any city or town in the state under Martial Law in fact without a public proclamation to that effect, and to deal with the lives, liberties and property of citizens as he may choose.

Section 10 gives the District Judges the power to command the state police and all sheriffs constables, deputies, city and town police, marshals or deputies within their several districts. This section transforms the civil judicial officer into a military officer —the peace officer into a war officer. This is unconstitutional, and were it not so, the condition of the country, the disposition, situation and circumstances of the people, render it unnecessary and improper. This unauthorized and unnecessary power enables the Judges to convert the courts of justice into political engines of oppression; and experience shows plainly that the judges of this administration are only too willing to use the power for that purpose. Courts of Justice ought to be in the midst of political commotions sure places of refuge for the innocent of every party, and should not be disgraced by wilder passions and fouler corruptions than are to be found on the hustings. The judges of our State are sufficiently prone to do wrong, without being aided by legislative enactments.

It was just such power as is here delegated to the Governor and the District Judges of the State, that developed and put in action the cruelty, and turned loose unrestrained the ferocious temper of Jeffreys upon the unprotected people of the Western district of England, known in history as the bloody District.

"Early in September," says Macaulay, "Jeffreys accompanied by four other judges set out on that circuit of which the memory will last as long as our race and language. The officers who accompanied the troops in the Districts through which his course lay had orders to *furnish him* with whatever military aid he might require. His ferocious temper needed no spur; yet a spur was applied."

We will not harrow up the minds of our readers by a recitation of the cruelties, outrages, murders, and inquisitorial torments inflicted on every class, age, and sex of the people of the districts through which he passed. These horrible murders and tortures could never have been inflicted had Jeffreys not had the power to call to his aid the military forces. He had the same power in this respect as that given by section 10 of the Police Bill to the District Judges of this State. He, we see, exercised his power to the fullest extent. And our Judges will exercise all the power granted them, and in many instances much more if not checked.

There is no denying the fact that we have some very willing *little* Jeffreys among the judiciary of the present administration, as we shall abundantly prove, when we come to review their acts.

We now come to consider the only other enactments of the Legislature in reference to the organization of the Governor's army approved April 12th 1871, and the amendment to the act approved July 1st 1871. The only significant feature in the Act of April 12th is that it enables all persons who are liable to serve in the Reserve Militia, to avoid such service by paying to the officer duly authorized to receive the same the sum of five dollars instead of fifteen as required by the 22 section of the Act of 24th of June 1870. It is apparent from these two sections that it was never the intention of the Governor (who recommends its enactment in these words, "It has been found in some states a good arrangement to embody a small force of the militia as may be willing to volunteer into a National Guard, and to aid the latter in arms and equipments by a levy of a tax on all persons liable to military duty who may by paying the same avoid enrollment") or of the Legislature that a militia force should be organized. They did not want citizens in their army. The passage of the 22 section in the original Act and the 22 section in the Act of 1871 was intended as invitations to the citizens of the state not to enroll in the militia (the last being of a more impressive nature than the first) as well as a means of obtaining a large sum of the people's money to be applied as the Governor suggests in his message.

By section 3rd of the Act of May 2, 1871 the Governor is enabled "to appoint any number of special police not to exceed twenty in each county in the State," or he may authorize their appointment. These special policemen shall only be paid when in actual service. Their compensation shall be three dollars per diem to be paid out of the county treasuries of the counties where employed on vouchers certified to by the Chief of Police.

These twenty special policemen were appointed in each county in the State twenty days before the close of the last election on the 6th October 1871, and were employed in riding through the counties with arms in hand for the purpose of compelling freedmen to come to the county seats and register, as well as to look them up and drive them to the polls to vote.

This sufficiently explains the object the administration had in view in passing the Act. Each of the One hundred and fifty-nine organized counties in the State has to pay for the services of these special policemen thus employed at every election and as much oftener as the Governor may choose to call them out the sum of One thousand and twenty-six dollars which for the State at large amounts to the sum of One hundred and sixty-three thousand one hundred and thirty four dollars. The people are not only to suffer the outrages and oppressions of the present administration, but are forced by Legislative enactments, to pay infamous men who are selected to oppress and defraud them.

We have frankly and honestly but briefly reviewed all the acts of the Legislature, which enable the chief Executive to organize, support and maintain a standing army in Texas, and at any and all times to control and direct its movements, which enable him to declare war against the people, for the declaration of Martial law, is in fact, a declaration of war.

Strange as it may appear, yet it is nevertheless a fact, that the Legislature has given his Exellency power, to declare war against the citizens, but in no legislative act has it given him the power to make peace, his war must therefore be a perpetual one, unless the humane Legislature interposes to stop it, for by the act, the Legislature alone can make peace. Why did they not confer this power upon the Governor? It may be they considered it a useless expenditure of the dear people's time, to confer the peace making power upon the Governor, being as intimately acquainted with him as they were.

To prove that the Governor is empowered to make war (declare Martial law) and not empowered to make peace, I have only to refer my readers to the 26th section of the act of 24th June 1870, commonly known as the Militia Bill, but more properly the *Governors Army Bill.*

We will for the present leave this branch of our review and not again refer to it until we come to review the manner in which the Governor exercised these extraordinary and unconstitutional powers.

We come now to consider as next in order, the act entitled "*an act to provide for the appointment by the Governor of certain officers to fill vacancies.*" The first section of this act proves the caption to be a base fraud instead of being an act, authorizing the Governor to fill vacancies, it is an an act confering on him the power to appoint officers, which by the plain letter of the constitution, are to be elected.

Section 1st makes it the duty of the Governor to appoint for each judicial district in this State, one district attorney who shall hold his office until the next general election in this State. This Section is grossly violative of Section 11th Article 5th of the State constitution, which reads "There shall be a district attorney elected by the qualified voters of each judicial district, who shall hold his office &c." Is it possible that the Legislature was so ignorant as not to discover the difference between the election of a district attorney "by the qualified voters of each judicial district" and the appointment of one by the Governor. But these worthy legislators may say that the office of district attorney was vacant throughout the State. Who made the office vacant? Tell the people why the office of district attorney was not filled at the general election in November 1869. It was not the fault of the constitution for it provided for their election nor was it the fault of the people. But because the office of district attorney was vacant, was no excuse for illegally filling it, when it might have been just as easily filled legally and constitutionally. An act might have been passed requiring the Governor to order an election to fill the vacancy. This would have been in harmony with the constitution and not violative of the spirit of our Republican institutions, but such a course would have defeated the designs and deep laid schemes of the Governor and the Legislature of robbing the people of their elective franchise, and of investing his Excellency with powers not conferred upon him by the constitution. The Legislature in this act, has bestowed upon the Governor a power reserved by the people to themselves.

Section 2nd authorized the Governor to appoint one County Treasurer and one County Surveyor for each County in the State, and all hide and cattle inspectors, and public weighers of cotton.

Section 3rd in some measure seems to conform to the caption, and grants to the Governor the power to appoint in each County in this State where a vacancy may exist by reason of the officer elect failing to take the oath prescribed by the act of Congress admitting Texas in the Union, approved March the 30th 1870, or failing to qualify in accordance with the laws of the State, or by death, resignation, or otherwise, one Sheriff and one district clerk." Unobservant readers might think this very fair and necessary to the due administration of justice, and to the prompt execution of the laws. But when it is read and considered in connection with the 5th Section of the Police Bill which enables the Governor to make the Sheriff's office vacant at will, it becomes obnoxious, and dangerous to the liberties of the people, and shows plainly that the intent of the Legislature was to concentrate all power in the hands of the Executive. Section 4th empowers the Governor to appoint a Mayor, and a board of Aldermen, or officers of like character, of such number as is or may be authorized by law, for each incorporated city and town in this State, and also a city recorder for each of the cities of Houston and Galveston, which officers shall hold their offices respectively, until the next general election in this State, or until otherwise provided by law. Here again is the concentration of more power in the Governor. Here the people (sometimes styled sovereigns) are divested of those powers and privileges which have been claimed and exercised heretofore by them, and which constitute the distinguishing features of our Republican form of government, what defeience or respect, we ask, is shown to the absolute sovereignty of the people, which is declared to be in them by the great declaration of American Independence, and which is a necessary element in all free and independent Republics, and without which they cannot exist.

It must be admitted that the people of the cities and towns of the State, are much more deeply and immediately interested and concerned, in procuring good, honest and efficient officers to rule over them, and are better enabled to judge of their qualifications and fitness for office, than the Governor, who is, from the very nature of the case in every or nearly every instance, a stranger to their condition, wants and necessities, and who has shown himself an unworthy repository of such power, by his partisan feelings in appointing only such to office, as are of his politics and obedient to his will, regardless of their qualifications.

This act enables the Governor to appoint nearly every officer known to the laws of the State, thereby placing in the hollow of his hand the life, liberty and property of every citizen in the State.

The acts confer a power and patronage on the Executive heretofore unknown in free Governments.

And what is very significant these powers were not conferred unasked. They were urged upon the Legislature by the Governor.

"Other subjects, (says his Excellency in his first message) must receive *immediate* attention as essential to the complete reorganization of the State Government, and among those which are of sufficient importance to require *special notice,* I will refer to the organization and appointment of Boards of Registry of voters, and of judges of elections; the appointment of officers to fill vacancies where the law or constitution does not now provide therefor; to provide for removals and appointments to municipal offices, until elections can be held in the respective cities and towns," &c. It would seem from this that the Legislature took the will of the Governor as its standard of right and wrong.

Every moderate man of both parties must be shocked by the insolence and perfidy of these Legislative enactments.

We have a parallel to this act in the reign of James II "all elections of Magistrates and of Towncouncils were prohibited; and the *King assumed* to himself the right of filling up the chief municipal offices." This is exactly what the Governor demanded of, and obtained from, the Legislature. The steps of the Legislature and of the Governor: to borrow the fine image of a Roman poet, are on the thin crust of ashes, beneath which the lava is still glowing.

We now come to the review of the act entitled *"an act to provide for the registration of voters"* approved July 11th 1870. This act like all the others of this administration, affecting the rights and liberties of the people, is covert, and to the casual or careless reader seems fair enough, but to those who are accustomed to read with great care, for the purpose of discovering the intent of the framers, They "are like unto white sepulchers which indeed appear beautiful outward but are within full of dead men's bones and of all uncleanness."

This act enables the Governor to appoint and remove at will all the registrars in the State, also the board of appeals and revision, who shall also be judges of elections. The 15th Section of this act gives to the board of appeals and revision throughout the State absolute and uncontrollable power over the franchise of the citizens.

"They shall decide says this section, the claims of all persons, who have been unable to appear before the registrar, and those of persons who consider that injustice has been done them by the registrar, and *shall strike from the lists of voters* the names of such as they shall consider improperly registered, and enter the names of such as they may consider improperly refused registration, and those who were unable to appear before the registrar, on the registration list." When we consider that there is no appeal from the decision of these three men, and no redress for the wrongs which they may inflict the power here becomes appalling Suppose they *shall consider* all citizens who are not of their politics improperly registered: what remedy have the citizens, they may appeal to the constitution in vain. They are answered by these men "that by a law of the Legislature we are the judges, and our decision is given you in the language of the act. "We consider you improperly registered and shall strike your names from the list of voters." Suppose they do this corruptly when the citizens are entitled to vote and offer to prove it by incontrovertible evidence; if after all this their names are stricken from the lists of registered voters. What penalty do these men incur under this law? None at all. This will plainly appear from an examination of the sections prescribing the punishment of the members of Boards of Appeal and judges of elections.

Section 25th.—Any judge of election, member of board of appeals, registrar, or clerk convicted of any offence under the next three succeeding sections shall be deemed guilty of a felony, and on conviction thereof, shall be punished by fine not exceeding one thousand dollars or by imprisonment in the penitentiary for not more than seven years." Section 26th describes the offences for which they shall be punished. Thus: "If any person shall alter, change, mutilate, or in any manner deface any book of registration, or shall take or carry away the same from the office of the clerk of the District Court Registrar or Judge of election or other place where the same may be lawfully deposited, or from the lawful possession of any person whomsoever, with intent to destroy, suppress, alter or conceal, or in any wise mutilate or destroy the same so as to prevent the lawful use of such book or books of registration, such persons shall be" &c. We see that this section does not define the offence of wilfully, or corruptly striking from the lists of voters the names of such as are properly registered. To alter, change, mutilate or deface any book of registration, neither of these constitutes the offence To take and carry away the registration book from the proper custodian, describes the offence whatsoever may be the intent with which it is done.

Section 28th punishes such persons as shall by threats, intimidation &c, disturb a registrar &c, in the discharge of their duties. These members of boards of appeals are not in this section liable to punishment for anything, much less for acting corruptly in striking names from the lists of voters. There is no penalty attached to this heinous crime, in this act or any other act of this 12th Legislature and if the offence was defined and the penalty affixed by the law, it would be inoperative because the law makes the members of the boards of appeals judges, with powers to pass upon, both the law, and the facts governing registration.

So it is with regard to registrars they cannot be punished under this act for registering persons not entitled to register, nor for refusing such as are lawfully entitled to register.

Section 1st of this act makes it the duty of the registrar, to register such persons as take the oath therein prescribed.

Section 13th of this act puts in the power of the registrar to reject even such as do take the oath prescribed in section 1st by giving him the power to examine under oath any person applying for registration, as to his qualification as a voter and permitting him dilligently to enquire into his qualifications, this section is not manditory but simply permissive. There is deep design in all this, and the facts prove that this power has been exercised in very many instances to deprive the citizen of his constitutional right to register and vote.

We will now examine the act entitled *"an act to provide for the mode and manner of conducting elections, making returns, and for the protection and purity of the ballot box,"* approved August 15th 1870. This act establishes the fact beyond cavil that the boards of appeal and revission, who are also judges of elections, may at their pleasure prevent citizens from voting.

Section 4th, of this act, reads when any person, whose name appears on the register, as that of one rejected as a voter, shall offer to vote, the judges of election shall, in addition to marking his ballot as rejected, keep the same separate from the ballots of qualified voters, so as effectually to prevent his vote from being counted as that of a qualified voter.

Section 5th makes it a personal offence in any Judge of election to receive or deposit the ballot of any person whose name does not appear upon the list of registered voters. We see by the 15th Section of the act of July 11th 1870 above referred to that the judges of election and boards of appeals and revision are composed of the same persons, and in that act they are enabled to strike from the list of voters the names of just such persons as they may think proper and no penalty attaches to them if they corruptly do it.

Section 7th provides that the first general election under this act shall be held on the first Tuesday after the first Monday in in November 1872, at which time and every two years thereafter members of Congress, Representatives and Senators to the State Legislature, District attorneys and all county officers made elective, shall be elected." The postponement of the general election by this act 'till December 1872 is an inexcusable violation of the 4th Section of Article III of the Constitution, which declares "that the members of the House of Representatives shall be chosen by the qualified electors, and their term of office shall be two years from the day of general election." The last general election under the present Constitution (at which the members of the 12th Legislature were elected) should have taken place on the first monday in July 1869, as appears from the "*Election* Declaration Section 1st included in the Constitution of the State and signed by Governor Davis as president of the Convention which formed the Constitution. Governor Davis and the Legislature ought therefore to have known that they violated the Constitution and disregarded the rights and wishes of the people of Texas in the passage of this 7th Section. The term of office of the 12th Legislature expired by limitation in July 1871, and by this Act one of the co-ordinate departments of the government is suspended and totally destroyed for the space of one year and five months. If the Legislature has the power to do this, may it not by the exercise of that same power do away with the Judicial department of the govenment, and concentrate *all* the powers of the government in the Executive department? which in fact they have nearly done. All acts passed by the 12th Legislature since July 1871, are by section 23rd of Article I of the Bill of Rights declared null and void. I will quote this section for the benefit of all whom it may concern, and for the information of the members of the 12th Legislature who voted for this Election Law, and for the Governor who approved it.

Section 23rd. "To guard against *transgressions* of the high powers herein delegated, we (the *people* of *Texas*) declare that *every thing* in this Bill of *Rights* is excepted out of the general powers of government and shall *forever remain inviolate;* and all *laws contrary* thereto, or to the *following provisions shall be void.*"

Why has the Legislature done this thing? "Why do the heathen rage and the people imagine a vain thing.

The Kings of the earth set themselves, and the rulers take counsel together against the Lord and against his annointed, saying Let us break their bonds assunder and cast away their cords from us.

He that sitteth in the heavens shall laugh; the Lord shall have them in derision, Be wise now. therefor, O ye kings; be instructed ye judges of the earth."

The Legislature has to a very alarming extent transferred the legislative powers of the government to the Executive, and we suppose it expects him to govern the people by proclamations until "the first Tuesday after the first Monday in December A. D. 1872, and then perhaps proclaim to the people of Texas that the day of election is indefinitely postponed, and to enforce this proclamation with the army by which it has surrounded him. The Governor by the 52nd Section of this Act, "shall on the days of the election have paramount charge and control of the peace and order of the State over all peace and police officers and shall have the command and direction in *chief* of all police officers by whomsoever appointed, and of all sheriffs and constables in their capacity as officers of the peace." This section gives the Governor the power to exercise a tremendous influence in the elections; and if he is so disposed he may effectually by force control them for partisan purposes.

We care not if the Governor be as just and as pure a man as was the immortal Washington, it would even then be wrong to place in his hands the power to destroy the liberties of the people, or such power as would enable him to take from them their rights or even curtail or infringe them.

" A just estimate, " says Washington, " of that love of power and proneness to abuse it which predominate in the human heart is sufficient to satisfy us of the truth of this position." Were this the only unwarranted and unnecessary power conferred by this Legislature upon the Governor we would not so much complain, but they have conferred upon him such a complete net-work of powers as renders his will absolute.

By section 21st of this Act the Judges of elections throughout the state are enabled effectually to prevent the people from reaping the benefits of their right to vote;—this they may accomplish by their mere written statement, " corroborated under oath by three respectable citizens, qualified electors of the county, " —they being the sole judges of the respectability of the three citizens. These three citizens may make oath to all this section requires (in order to throw out the vote) and swear truly, and yet there may have been a fair election. Let's examine into this —suppose " *during* the time of election (to use the language of this section) at any place at or, near any poll or voting place, " there should be (in the estimation of these judges and three citizens) a *riot* or tumult, or acts of violence or intidimation, or armed disturbance, or bribery or corrupt influence which shall prevent, *or tend* to *prevent* a fair (or) free (or) peaceable and full vote of all the qualified electors of said county. " You will see from this that the judges of election are only to make the statement and the three citizens to corroborate it under oath, that these acts or either one of them "*tend* to prevent a fair, full, peaceable and full vote of all qualified voters of said county. They are not required by the section to swear that these acts or either of them *did actually* prevent a fair, free, peaceable and full vote

Suppose there should be a tumult or riot at or near the polls or voting place on the days of election, and suppose that riot tends to, but does not in fact, prevent a fair free and full vote, ought the vote at that box for this reason to be thrown out? And should any man or set of men be enabled by law under such a state of facts to throw them out? Every honest minded man will at once say no,—because this would put it in the power of a few wicked, corrupt and designing men at every election throughout the state to defeat the will of the people, which, we trust was not the design of this section. Yet by Section 25th of this Act, the returning officers may upon the statement of these judges of election corroborated by the affidavit of the three citizens in form as required in the 21st Section of this Act *pass upon* and *refuse* "*to canvass or compile* the statement of the votes at such poll or voting place, and exclude it from their returns." This shows how hard it is for the people of Texas who are opposed to the oppressive policy of the present administration to get to vote and get their votes fairly counted and returned;—but don't despair, —the day of our deliverance is not far distant. Does it not strike the reader as being rather singular, that in all elections which have been held during the present administration, that the votes at the polls or voting places which gave the administration party the majority, have not in a single instance been thrown out, and that the votes at so many polls or voting places which gave large majorities against the administration party have been thrown out? Why is this? Let the Governor and his hired tools answer this question, for they know! If the real object of the Legislature in passing this Act had been "the protection and purity of the ballot box" they might have effectually accomplished this by establishing a poll or voting place in each justice's precinct in the several counties throughout the state which would have greatly lessened the inconveniences of the people, and prevented the assembling of such immence crowds of men at the county seats which the present law necessitates, and would have destroyed whatever tendency might exist towards *riot* or tumult, or acts of violence, or intimidation or armed disturbance, and greatly facilitated a *fair, free*, peaceable and full vote of all the qualified electors. The enactment of such a law was contemplated by the Seventh section of Article III, of the State Constitution, which declares that "all elections for state, district or county officers, shall be held at the county seats of the several counties *until otherwise provided by law*."

We will now glance for a moment at the Act entitled "*An Act to provide for the protection of the frontier*.

There is no class of our fellow citizens who more justly deserve and merit the aid and sympathy of the whole people of Texas than our exposed and unprotected frontiersmen, and we would not by word or deed throw a straw in the way of their complete protection. But it is not even to be hoped that they will be protected by the enforcement of this act.

The most effectual, if not indeed the only way the frontier can be protected is to permit the people on the frontier to raise companies of rangers among themselves and to select their own officers, from such men as are known and tried Indian hunters. If the government will do this and pay the Rangers well for their services, in a short time the people on the frontier will feel secure in their homes and property. By this Act the Governor is to raise and muster into the service of the State for the protection of the Northern and Western frontier twenty companies of Texas Rangers to consist of one Captain, one Lieutenant, one medical officer, three sergeants, four corporals, one bugler, one farrier (what does a company of frontier stock raisers want with a farrier ?) and fifty privates..

By section three of the Act the Governor appoints the Captains of companies to enroll the requisite number of men for the companies, and when as many as fifty men shall have been enrolled for any one company said company shall organize by holding an election for Lieutenant. This is all wrong, each company should have had the privilege of selecting their commanding officer, and this Act ought to require the officers at least to be frontiersmen. By section 12 the Governor appoints the officer to command and direct the movements of the whole twenty companies. This is wrong, and bad policy, if the protection of the frontier is the main object.

The management of the entire force raised under the provisions of this act shall be at all times *under* and *subject* to the order of the Governor. These twenty companies constitute the third wing of the Governor's army. If this organization has in the slightest degree rendered the people of the frontier any protection we have yet to learn the fact; and if it ever does give them security and protection we will be most agreeably disappointed.

We will review in connection with the foregoing act an act entited "*an Act providing for the issuance and sale of the bonds of the State for the purpose of meeting the appropriation made for maintaining Ranger Companies on the frontier.*" Section 1st of this Act provides for the issuance and sale by the Governor of seven hundred and fifty thousand dollars of the bonds of the State of Texas bearing seven per cent interest per annum, the interest payable semi-annually in gold on the 1st day of September and March of each year. By section second said bonds are to be issued under the direction of the Governor, and are to be redeemable at the pleasure of the State after *twenty* years, and payable forty years from date." This places more power in the Governor by placing the money of the people at his disposal.

The following figures will show whether or not this financial arrangement will result in benefit to the people of the State.

Let us suppose the Governor sells these bonds for seventy-five cents on the dollar, the State will then realize from their sale the sum of five hundred and sixty-two thousand dollars in currency; deduct from this amount one per cent allowed the agent for selling, and two thousand dollars for engraving and printing and we have left five hundred and fifty three thousand dollars in currency as the net proceeds of the sale of the bonds. The people pay annually on these bonds as interest fifty two thousand five hundred dollars in gold. If the bonds are redeemed in twenty years the people will then have paid in interest, one million and sixty thousand dollars in gold. Add this amount to seven hundred and fifty thousand dollars (the amount necessary to redeem the bonds) and the State will have paid in gold *One million eight hundred thousand dollars*, and will have received in lieu of that enormous sum five hundred and fifty three thousand dollars in currency, and if the bonds are not redeemed for forty years, the State will have paid in gold for five hundred and fifty three thousand dollars in currency the round sum of three million six hundred thousand dollars in gold. It will not take many such enactments as this to bankrupt the State.

As we are upon the subject of bonds we had as well review the Act approved May 19th 1871, and entitled "*an Act to authorize the Governor to prepare and issue bonds to an amount sufficient to meet any deficiency in the receipts of revenue for the years* 1871 *and* 1872, *and also providing for the payment of said bonds and interest thereon.*"

By section 1st the Governor is empowered to have printed or engraved an amount of bonds not to exceed in value four hundred thousand dollars, with coupons bearing ten per cent, per annum interest, to supply any deficiency of the revenue for the current and ensuing year and to meet appropriations for support of the State Government and other purposes."

The people of Texas who pay the taxes, we are disposed to think, have long since come to the conclusion that the various and burdensome taxes which they are now required to pay ought to be sufficient to defray all the legitimate expenses of the government. If the government is now borrowing money at a high rate of interest, or what is still worse, selling the bonds of the State at any discount, and paying ten per cent, per annum interest on them to meet the current expenses, daily increasing, it is very evident that in order to meet this additional indebtedness the present rate of taxes will have to be increased to such an extent as will completely exhaust the resources of the people. By section 2d of this Act these bonds are to be paid in lawful money of the United States (Currency) the interest coupons thereon to be paid semi-annually on the 1st day of September and March of each year, and to be redeemable at the pleasure of the State after two years, and payable five years after date. The Governor is to sell the bonds and receive the money. Suppose he sells them for eighty cents on the dollar, they will bring three hundred and sixty thousand dollars, deduct from this amount four thousand dollars which is allowed the Governor by the act for selling, fifteen hundred dollars for engraving and printing the same, which leaves three hundred and fifty four thousand five hundred dollars net proceeds. The people have to pay in interest each year upon these bonds the sum of forty thousand dollars. If the State is able to redeem the bonds in five years, the people will have paid in interest above, two hundred thousand dollars. Add this to the amount required to redeem the bonds and the people will have paid six hundred thousand dollars. Add to this amount the debt created by the sale of the bonds under the Act of August 5th 1870, three million six hundred thousand dollars in gold, and the tax payers of the State will have paid from their hard earnings, and we fear in very many instances from the sale of their property by the sheriff, the sum of four million five hundred thousand dollars; and the state will have received in lieu of this amount the sum of nine hundred and eleven thousand dollars to be applied to defraying the expenses of the government.

At the present prodigal rate of expenditure, when will the people be able to pay this debt? By the last section of this act the Legislature declared the Act *"to be irrepealable in any of its provisions* till principal and interest of said bonds are fully paid."

How absurd this declaration!

Is it possible that this Legislature has arrogated to itself the power to bind all future Legislatures in the State? There never did, there never will, and there never can exist a Legislature possessed of the *right* or *power* of binding and controlling future Legislatures. They had just as well declare that Edmund J. Davis shall govern the State of Texas till the *day* of *judgment.* All such Acts by which the makers of them attempt to do what they have neither the power nor the right to do, nor the power to execute are in themselves null and void. This Legislature assumes to itself the power to *enact* Constitutions for the people of Texas as well as laws. In an act entitled "an act to prevent the cessation of judicial functions &c," approved June 18th, 1870, page 10 the Legislature declares in section 2 "that the Supreme Judges are authorized and required to proceed in the discharge of their respected functions until appointments shall be made by the Governor, according to the *Constitution and laws to be enacted by the Legislature.*

But we may be told that this is a misprint; why should this be a misprint any more than the *irrepealable* Act? it is much less absurd and easier to be executed. But we are told that the irrepealable Act conforms to the 23 section of Act XII of the Constitution. It violates that clause of the Constitution. The Constitution declares that *"it shall* be the duty of the Legislature to provide by law in all cases when State or County debt is created adequate means for the payment of the current interest, and *two per cent* as a sinking fund for the redemption of the principal; and all *such* laws shall be irrepealable until principal and interest are fully paid. The *irrepealable* law above referred to is not *such* a law as the Constitution defines. This Act makes no provision for a sinking fund of *two* per cent for the redemption of the principal but requires that thirty three and one third per cent shall be paid on the bonds annually when they become redeemable. Does the Constitution authorize the Legislature to declare this provision irrepealable? No! It does seem that the 12th Legislature has passed no law, all the provisions of which conformed to the Constitution. As it is not our purpose in this review to point out objections to the Constitution, we will leave this subject to the reflection of the reader.

Again, by the Act approved December 2nd, 1871, entitled "*an Act authorizing a loan to meet deficiencies in the revenue of the State,*" the Governor is authorized to have engraved the bonds of the State of Texas to the amount of two million of dollars, first, one million in bonds of the denomination of one thousand dollars each; second, five hundred thousand dollars in bonds of the denomination of five hundred dollars each; Third, five hundred thousand dollars in bonds of the denomination of one hundred dollars each.

Said bonds shall be payable twenty years from the date thereof, and shall bear interest at the rate of seven per cent per annum payable semi-annually, viz: on the first day of January and the first day of July of each year. Said bonds to have coupons attached for each installment of interest which may become due. The principal and interest of said bonds shall be payable in gold at the treasury of the State of Texas, or at the city of New York through such agent or agents as the Governor may select to pay the same. Said bonds shall be signed by the Governor and Treasurer of the State, and countersigned and registered by the Comptroller with the seal of the State of Texas affixed thereto. The Governor appoints the agent to sell the bonds in the city of New York at such times and in such quantities as he may direct. The amount to be paid for these bonds is left discretionary with the Governor. He may sell them at par, or for five cents on the dollar. Neither he nor such agents as he may appoint are required to give bond to secure the payment of the money into the Treasury of the State after the bonds shall have been sold. To say the least, this is placing before the Governor and his agents a very great temptation. The Legislature before it passed this act should have read that part of the Lord's prayer which says "*lead us not into temptation.*"

Suppose the Governor sells these bonds for eighty cents on the dollar. They will bring one million six hundred thousand dollars, deduct from this amount one per cent for selling and five thousand dollars appropriated for engraving, and we have as net proceeds of the sale of the bonds, one million five hundred and seventy-five thousand dollars in currency. The people of the State will have to pay annually the sum of one hundred and forty thousand dollars in gold as interest on these bonds which will amount in twenty years to two million eight hundred thousand dollars, which added to the bonds sold creates a debt against the State of four million eight hundred thousand dollars, add to this, four million two hundred thousand dollars in gold the debt created under the Acts of August 5th, 1870, May 19th, 1871, and the State debt is increased to nine million of dollars, provided the interest and principal be not paid And at the present rate of expenditure it will be impossible to meet the interest of this debt without additional taxation. And Governor Davis must be considered the "Keystone" of this combination, "the life and blood of this conspiracy" to bankrupt the State and oppress the people with taxes, taxes, taxes too grevious to be borne. In his message to the Senate and House of Representatives of January 10th, 1871, he recommends the passage of these very laws. He says "there must however be a revenue provided sufficient for the just necessities of the government, and the only question to be solved relates to its assessment in the manner least oppressive to the poor and so as to prevent evasion."

Here the Governor draws a distinction between the rich and the poor of the State. Does he mean to say that a man once poor, who has by the sweat of his brow and by strict economy and self denial accumulated property, thereby places himself beyond the protection of the law, and becomes a legitimate subject for oppressive taxation? The Governor in fact says that *the only* questions to be solved relates to its assessment in the manner *most oppressive to the rich.* The Constitution requires taxation to be *equal* and uniform throughout the State. The Governor had an object in view when he used this language; and that object was not in fact the relief of the poor, as we shall show when, we consider the effect of heavy taxation upon the poor man whether he have or have not property to be directly taxed. The oppression comes on him, and he feels it, but it comes in a disguised form.

We will now review the Act entitled "*an act to provide for the payment of the public debt of the State of Texas*" *approved May 2nd* 1871.

By this Act the Attorney General, Comptroller of Public Accounts and State Treasurer are constituted an additional board of which the Attorney General is the president and legal adviser. It is made the duty of this board to examine all claims for money against the State reported on by the board organized under the provisional Act of November 9th 1866 and the amount of indebtedness on account of the penitentiary incurred under competent authority, and to admit and allow all of such claims as to them appear just and valid claims against the state, and were authorized by preexisting laws, and are not inconsistent with the Constitution of the State. This board shall by its president endorse on said bond or bonds that they are valid and on presentation at the treasury the same shall be paid. This Act only permits the additional board to examine and endorse as valid the claims for money against the state reported on by the board organized under the Act of November 1866, and the amount of indebtedness on account of the penitentiary. The Governor by this Act is authorized to procure the means to pay off the indebtedness as ascertained by the report of this additional board, by the issue and sale of six per cent coupon bonds of the state payable in Twenty years—interest payable semi-annually at the treasury. The Governor is made the agent of the State to sell or otherwise dispose of the bonds. We urge no objection to this;—but we have grave objections to urge against the Act entitled "*An Act supplemental to this act* approved May 22nd 1871.

This supplemental act gives the auditorial board in addition to the powers granted in the above act the power to audit and allow all the claims that may appear to them just and valid claims against the State. And the board shall by its president endorse on said bond or claims that they are valid; and on presentation of the same at the treasury, the same shall be paid when due, and for this purpose fifty thousand dollars are appropriated provided that all allowances of claims against the State shall be subject to the approval of the Governor before becoming valid claims against the state. These two acts enable the auditorial board and the Governor to say what the debt of the State is or shall be, and the Governor is authorized to issue and sell the bonds of the State to discharge the indebtedness. Suppose the Governor should organize an army of one hundred thousand men in addition to the army already organized and keep them in service two years, and present a claim of ten million of dollars against the state to this additional board, what in this Act would prevent them from "auditing and allowing the claim"? They are commanded by this supplemental Act to audit and allow all claims that may appear to them just and valid claims against the state and authorized by preexisting laws.

There is a preexisting law which enables the Governor to organize as many troops in Texas as he may think proper under the name of State Guard, Militia Bill Section 3rd, and he has "*power to negotiate with the government of the United States for the loan or purchase of arms for the use of the military force of this State*, Ib. Section 23rd.

This law provides that these troops shall be paid. If this auditorial board "*audit and allow claims against* the state" which are not just, to whom are they responsible? To no one but themselves. If the Governor issues and sells the bonds of the State to discharge invalid claims, to whom is he responsible? to *himself alone.*

The Legislature fraudulently and illegally elected as it was, is nevertheless supposed to hold the purse of the State in *trust* for the State; but in the manner in which this Legislature has acted "it is like a man being both mortgagor and mortgagee, and in the case of misapplication of trust it is the criminal sitting in judgment upon himself. If those who vote the supplies are the same persons who received the supplies when voted, and are to account for the expenditure of those supplies to those who voted them it is *themselves accounting to themselves*, and the Comedy of Errors concludes with the Pantomime of *Hust.*"

While we are upon this subject of money perhaps it would be appropriate to review the *Tax* laws passed during the present administration.

"*An act to levy taxes.*"

In order that our readers may the better understand the rapid increase of taxes under the present administration, we will quote one section from the law passed in 1870, and several sections from the act of 1871 approved April 22nd.

Section 1st. There shall be levied and collected for the use and support of the State, on all property real and personal, a direct advalorum tax of one third of one per centum on the 1st of January 1871 and on that day in every year thereafter.

An Act to give effect to the several provisions of the Constitution concerning Taxes.

Section 1st That each and all of the several provisions of the Constitution concerning taxes shall have force and effect according to their terms and as hereinafter enacted and the following enumerated annual taxes for each successive year including the present year are levied and imposed, and are to be assessed collected and applied as hereby prescribed.

Section 2nd. An annual poll tax of one dollar on all male persons in this State between the ages of twenty one and sixty years for the benefit of the public school.

The direct advalorum State Tax.

Section 3rd. An annual direct *advalorum* State tax of one half of one per centum of the cash value thereof estimated in lawful coin of the United States on all real property situated and personal property owned in this State, save so much thereof as may be exempted from taxation by the laws of this State or of the United States—one fourth for the benefit of public schools, and three fourths for the support of the State government, and for such other purposes as may be by law directed.

The direct advalorum county tax.

Section 4th. An annual direct advalorum county tax of one half of the above mentioned rate of taxation on all real property situate, and all personal property owned in each county in this state, save so much thereof as is exempted from taxation, as aforesaid, for the support of the several county organizations thereof, and for such other pubic purposes as the court thereof may order. This tax, if deemed too large, may before the collection thereof be reduced to any specific less rate by order of the county court.

Section 5th. An annual direct advalorum tax of one fourth of one per centum shall be levied on the value of all property subject to taxation thereby for public roads and bridges, to be applied by the County Courts, subject to such regulations as the Legislature may prescribe, also an annual poll tax of not less than one dollar upon each and every male person over twenty one years of age, to be imposed at the discretion of each county court, respectively, any person thus taxed having the option of working upon said roads or bridges at the rate of one dollar per day.

The occupation Tax.

Section 6th. There shall be levied on and collected from every person, firm or association of persons, pursuing any of the following named occupations an annual tax (except when herein otherwise provided) on every such occupation and separate establishment as follows:

1st. For selling spirituous, vinous, malt or other intoxicating liquors in quantities less than a quart.......$150.00

2nd. For every billiard, bagatelle, pigeon hole, or Jenny Lind table.. 25.00

3rd. For every mine or ten pin alley within any incorporated city or town used for profit..................... 200.00

4th. For every nine or ten pin alley beyond the limits of any incorporated city or town or county site used for profit.. 100.00

5th. For every foot peddler in each and every county.. 10.00

6th. For every one horse peddler or a peddler with one yoke of oxen.. 25.00

7th. For every peddler with two horses or two yoke of oxen 50.00

8th. For every gift enterprise 500.00

9th. For every theatre or dramatic representation for which pay for admittance is demanded or received for each representation thereof 5.00

10th. For every circus, for each performance 25.00

11th. For every menagerie, wax work or exhibition of any kind, every day 5.00

12th. For every concert for money 5.00

13th. For every hotel in any city or town of three thousand inhabitants or more 50.00

14th. For one less than three and more than one thousand 25.00

15th. And for all other Hotels 15.00

16th. For any cook shop, eating house or boarding house 15.00

17th. For any livery stable in any city or town of five thousand inhabitants or more 50.00

18th. In one of less than five and more than three thousand inhabitants 25.00

19th. In one of less than three and more than one thousand inhabitants 10.00

20th. And for all other livery stables 5.00

21st. For every distillery 100.00

22nd. For every brewery 50.00

23rd. For every whole sale merchant 150.00

24th. For every first class retail merchant 100.00

25th. " " Second " " " 50.00

26th. " " Third " " " 25.00

27th. " " Fourth " " " 10.00

28th. " " traveling agent selling patent rights or patent specific medicines 50.00

29th. For every person or firm dealing in stocks or Bills of Exchange in any city or town exceeding five thousand in population... 250.00

30th. And from any such person or firm in any city or town of less than five thousand inhabitants............... 50.00

31st. For every life insurance company doing business in this state.. 500.00

32nd. For every fire and marine insurance company doing business in this state.................................. 250.00

33rd. From every physician surgeon or dentist........ 10.00

34th. Every attorney at law............................... 10.00

35th. From every daguerreanist in a town or city of of less than five thousand inhabitants......................... 25.00

36th. If more than five thousand inhabitants.......... 50.00

37th. For every auctioneer................................. 5.00

38th For every Barber for each chair....................... 5.00

39th. " " person or firm following the occupation of ship, merchandise or cotton broker.................... 40.00

40th. For every pawnbroker............................. 30.00

41st. From every keeper of public ferry................ 10.00

42nd. " " " " toll bridge.................. 10.00

43rd. " " person or firm buying or selling upon Commission.. 50.00

44th. From every land agent................................ 10.00

The County Courts of the several counties of this state shall have the power of levying taxes equal to one half of the amounts herein levied.

45th. There shall be levied on, and collected from any and all Railroad and Telegraph companies doing business in this State an annual tax of one per centum upon the net receipts of the same."

The subject of taxation deeply and directly affects the interest and prosperity of every man who by industry, frugality and application to business has accumulated property, it also very materially affects such as have no property and who are forced to gain a livelihood for themselves and families by the daily labor of their hands.

Heavy taxation reduces the rich to poverty, and prevents the poor from becoming rich.

It not only affects the present generation of tax payers, but to a greater or less degree their children, for if their father is broken up by excessive taxation, it disables him from giving his sons and daughters those advantages so essential to their happiness and success in life, and leaves him powerless to render them aid, and forces them to commence the battle of life with no capital, but physical strength. It deeply affects the industry of the country, breaks the spirit of the people, and renders them less able to meet its demands. It renders the people discontented, and makes them dissatisfied with the government, which in turn weakens its power and brings it into contempt.

We see that the first tax law passed during the present administration (which we will herein designate as the law of 1870) provides for the levy and collection on all property real and personal, a direct advalorum tax of one third of one per cent, which is thirty three and one third cents on the one hundred dollars worth of property, also a poll tax of one dollar. By section 7th, the Police court has power to levy (for county purposes) taxes equal to one half of the State tax. By the Act approved April 22nd 1871, the direct *advalorum* state tax is increased to one half of one per cent, which is fifty cents upon every one hundred Dollars worth of property in the State—by this Act the county Courts, are authorized to levy a direct *advalorum* county tax, and in addition to that a direct *advalorum* Road and bridge tax of one fourth of one per centum on all real and personal property around or situated in the county; in addition to this the State levies an occupation tax, and the county courts levy an occupation tax of one half the amount of the State occupation tax. The justices of the peace receive five per cent as commissions for assessing the taxes, which is added in each assessment and paid by the property owner.

We will now show by figures what this tax all amounts to.

We will take a first class retail merchant. First he pays an occupation tax of one hundred dollars. Second a poll tax of one dollar. Third, his *advalorum* State tax. We will estimate his lots and store house at fifteen thousand dollars;—his *advalorum* state tax on that amount is seventy five dollars per annum, suppose he sells during the year one hundred thousand dollars worth of goods—his State *advalorum* tax on them amounts to five hundred dollars, his tax for district school houses is one fourth the amount of the direct *advalorum* State tax which on his real and personal property would amount to one hundred and forty three dollars, and seventy five cents. This foots up eight hundred and nineteen dollars and seventy five cents, add to this amount five per cent for commissions to the justice of the peace for assessing state tax and five per cent on all this for frontier protection, and we have nine hundred and one dollars and seventy five cents, the merchant's State tax. We will now see what his county tax foots up. Poll tax one dollar. His county *advalorum* tax on his house and lot and goods amounts to three hundred and ninety five dollars and eighty six cents. His direct *advalorum*, road and bridge tax of one fourth of one per centum on his real and personal property amounts to three hundred and seventy five dollars.

His occupation tax is fifty dollars. This for county Tax foots up eighteen hundred and thirty nine dollars and twenty eight cents. Add five per cent of that amount for commissions for assessing, and we have the merchants total county tax eight hundred and eighty one dollars and twenty four cents, which added to the state tax we have one thousand seven hundred and eighty three dollars and four cents. When he pays this, the State and county let him go, instantly the Corporate authorities seize him, and he is required to pay an annual tax of one half of one per cent upon his property in the corporation, which would amount to seven hundred and fifty dollars. This swells his taxes to two thousand five hundred and thirty three dollars and four cents.

Is this all? no, no, as soon as he gets free from the marshall he is accosted by a finely dressed stranger who very politely informs him that he is a collector of the United States Internal Revenue Tax and would be pleased to receive the tax due upon his income,—and he receives from the merchant a tax of five per cent on his income which on ten thousand dollars, is five hundred. This amount and the others added make his entire taxes amount to three thousand and thirty three dollars and four cents.

And this is not all. The present administration is at this *moment* forcing from the people, a tax of Seven Eights of one per centem—on all the real and personal property owned in the State for the ostensible purpose of building School houses. This would swell the merchants tax—to Four Thousand thirty nine dollars and twenty nine cents($4,039.29) all of which amount ultimately comes out of the pockets of the producing classes, who are forced to purchase and consume the merchants goods. We from hence see that taxation is a many sided burden. It burdens the people by lessening the value of their property, and by increasing the value of the articles which they are compelled to purchase for consumption, thereby rendering them less able to meet it.

The Legislature by one part of this law, has increased the expenses of living and have taken away the means by another.

The laboring man is not sensible of the weight of the tax which this law imposes upon him, because it is disguised to him in the articles which he buys, and he thinks only of their dearness. He finds the prices of sugar, coffee, bread, clothing, and every other article which he must buy for the support and comfort of his family, so high that it requires the hardest labor and strictest economy on his part to enable him to live at all, and still he discovers not the cause. The present taxes take from him at least one fourth part of his yearly earnings; he is consequently disabled from providing for a family, especially if he or any of them are afflicted with sickness. The money arising from these taxes ought to be touched with the most scrupulous consciencieousness of honor. It is not the produce of riches only, but of the hard earnings of labor and poverty. It is drawn even from the bitterness of want and misery. Not a beggar passes or perishes in our cities whose mite is not in that mass.

The tax on the various other occupations named in the Act is as high and in many instances higher than on that of the merchants. By the tax law passed during Gov. Throckmorton's administration in 1866 the annual advalorum State tax was only fifteen cents on the one hundred dollars worth of property, and that of the county seven and a half cents on the one hundred dollars worth of property, making in all twenty-two and one half cents on the one hundred dollars worth of property, which was sufficient to meet all the expenses of the government, whereas by the tax law of the present administration, the advalorum state and county tax amounts to two dollars and fifty two and one half cents. The stock raiser's tax amounts to four dollars and seventy seven cents upon the hundred dollars, and withal the State is contracting debts. The appropriations made by the Legislature for the present administration already foot up Five million four hundred and fifty four thousand and five hundred and ninety five dollars ($5.454.595) and to day there is not a cent in the Treasury. The appropriations during Governor Throckmorton's administration for the same length of time were $930.350 .77 and when he was removed there was a considerable sum of money in the Treasury.

By section 19 of the act of 1871, any tax on personal property due and unpaid may be collected by the sheriff or his deputy by levying thereon, and he may sell the same by advertising as in case of personal property levied upon under execution.

The collection of this tax will create great distress throughout the State and excite discontent in the minds of the people.

The poorer classes of the people will frequently be unable to pay this tax when it becomes due. When this happens the Sheriff or his deputy will visit their homes and seize and carry away such property as he can lay his hands on. The cow which furnishes his babe with milk will be driven away and sold under the Sheriff's hammer for a song. If this does not satisfy the demand for taxes the single bed of the poor family, may be carried away and sold. The tears of the distressed mother and her helpless children will have no effect on the rapacious tax gatherers.

"Like plundering soldiers they'd enter the door,
And make a distress on the goods of the poor,
While frightened poor children distractedly cried :
This nothing abated their insolent pride."

The oppressions from these heavy taxes are not yet as fully felt by the people, as they will be, after they have continued a year or two, and the officers have enforced their collections by seizure and sale; or as fully as they will be when the fellow statute is put in vigorous force.

Section 1st. That every person or member of a firm or corporation subject to the payment of an occupation tax who shall neglect or fail after having been duly notified by any officer charged with the collection of any such occupation tax to comply with any one of the several provisions of an act entitled "an Act to give effect to the several provisions of the Constitution concerning taxes, approved April 22, 1871 concerning occupation tax shall be deemed guilty of a misdemeanor, and shall on conviction, on indictment, or information be punished by fine not less than five nor more than one hundred dollars."

And by section 2nd of this Act it is made a penal offence for the officer who is charged with the collection of this tax, not to indict such as fail to pay the tax. This simply means that if the poor man is unable to pay an occupation tax, he is prohibited from pursuing the occupation, though it be his only means of making a living, and if he does pursue it, he becomes indebted to the State, and if that indebtedness is not discharged by payment when it becomes due, the State prosecutes him, and puts him in jail until he pays the tax, and also the fine and costs of the prosecution. This is in direct violation of the 15th section of the Bill of Rights, which declares that *"no person shall ever be imprisoned for debt."*

This will convince the people of the necessity of reform and a change in the officers who administer the affairs of the government.

It is time indeed that the people of Texas should be rational, and not be governed like animals for the pleasure of their riders.

We ought to have pride or shame enough to blush at being thus imposed upon, and when we feel our proper character, we will.

Upon all subjects of this nature there is often passing in the mind a train of ideas which we have not yet accustomed ourselves to encourage and communicate. Restrained by something which puts on the character of prudence we act the hypocrite upon ourselves as well as to others. It is however curious to observe how soon this spell can be dissolved. A single expression boldly conceived and uttered will sometimes put a whole company into their proper feeling; and whole states and whole nations are acted upon in the same manner.

No reform in this or any other respect is to be looked for from the present administration, and whenever it does come it must come from the people and not from the government. At the next election the people will reform these laws. They will speak, though hell itself should gape and bid them hold their peace.

We will next consider the act entitled "*an act regulating public printing.*"

The first objection we urge to this Act is that the rates paid the public printer are exorbitant. He receives for printing the laws of a general and special nature including the index one fourth of a cent per page; for printing one thousand copies of the Journals of each House, one fourth of a cent per page. For printing eight hundred copies of the Governor's message &c one third of a cent per page. For two hundred copies of bills and resolutions three dollars and fifty cents per page and for each additional one hundred copies two dollars and fifty cents per page. For all rule and figure work he receives double the above rates. For all laws of a general and special nature, joint resolutions, proclamations of the Governor, and other public documents one dollar per square of ten lines nonpareil. Such prices as above will make any public printer immensely rich in one year. This is one of the many ways in which the people's money is squandered. Section 13 of the act empowers the Governor to designate certain journals to perform and publish the county and judiciary advertising of the Judicial Districts respectively in which such journals may be published, and if no journal is published in any judicial district in this State the publication may be made in a paper published nearest thereto. And this Act requires that all printing and advertising for or in any judicial district shall be done by and published in the journal designated by the Governor as the journal for the district. This section places very great power in the hands of the Governor to be used for political purposes.

It is an absolute fraud upon the people to require all judicial advertisements to be made in the official organs. If an administrator in Brown County for instance, wishes to sell the property of the estate he represents, he must have the sale advertised in Austin, at heavy cost and it is more than probable that not a single man who attends the sale will ever have seen the paper in which the notice of sale was required by law to be published, and the proceeds arising from the sale of the property of the estate may not be sufficient to pay for the advertisement. This is all wrong and unjust and burdensome to the people. They get no equivalent for the money they are forced to spend in this way, in a majority of the instances. And what is still worse it presses hardest upon the poor widows and orphans of the State. The greater portion of the small patrimony which is left them, generally finds its way into the pockets of the editor of one of these judicial organs.

One other and very strong objection to this law, is that it adds to the already excessive patronage of the Governor. This act gives him absolute power over thirty-five printing presses in the State.

He has power over the support of the individuals who run them. He makes and unmakes them. His spirit animates their actions. He selects them from among his friends and supporters, and may dismiss them and will as often as they disappoint his expectations. All these organs derive all or nearly all their support from the government patronage. Here we see that government patronage is distributed for party purposes. Under such a state of facts it is impossible for any government to maintain integrity. This government is manufacturing a poison which will destroy its lifeblood. Every office in the State is a bribe which perverts and corrupts the man who holds it and the man who gives it. No man is honest who aids and abets any party or set of men to destroy the liberties of the people for the sake of personal advantage. Yet we find that there are always plenty to be found who will accept the offices created by the government, at any sacrifice of honor and manhood provided there be *money in them.*

We will next consider the act entitled "*an act to establish a system of public free schools for the State of Texas, approved Aug. 13th* 1870.

Before we examine this statute we will say that the people of Texas have at all times been in favor of a free school system, and to day are in favor of a system which will include within the pale of its benefits and influence every child in Texas white and black between the ages of eight and eighteen years. Who does not believe that it is the duty of government to provide for the instruction of all youth? and that this instruction should not be left to chance or charity but should be secured by law?

We hold that for the purpose of public instruction every man should be subject to taxation in proportion to his property whether he himself have or have not children to be benefitted by the education for which he pays. Such we declare to be a wise and liberal policy by which property and life and the peace of society are secured. By inspiring a wholesome and conservative principle of virtue and knowledge in our youth, we will do much to prevent the extension of crime. Education excites a feeling of respectability and a sense of character while at the same time it enlarges the capacity and increases the sphere of intellectual enjoyment. By this general instruction we will in a great measure purify the whole moral atmosphere. If, indeed, our government *does* rest upon the *will of the people*, in order to protect and perpetuate it, we must give the public will the proper direction by education. By the diffusion of general knowledge and good and virtuous sentiments, our political fabric may be secure, as well against open violence and overthrow, as against the insidious and sure undermining of licentiousness and vice. If the States in which a large number of the members of the present Legislature were raised, had a good free school system established by law, we would find among them less licentiousness and a greater regard for the constitutional rights of the people, and some of that manliness and independence of character which elevate men above the atmosphere of evil passions and party prejudice. Had such been the case their legislation would have been a blessing to the State instead of a curse. It would have united the discordant elements, allayed whatever animosity may have existed, imbued the minds of the people with confidence and respect for the government by assuring them that they should reap and enjoy unmolested the fruits of their toil and industry. Our first objection to this school law is that it places too much power and patronage in the hands of the Governor. The Governor by and with the advice and consent of the Senate appoints the superintendent of Public Instruction, who is to continue in office until the first general election, then he is to be elected. He holds his office for four years.

Our second objection is, that it neither requires the Superintendent to give bond or take the oath of office. This act of 1870 is much less objectionable than that of 1871.

By section 3rd of the former Act each organized county in the state constituted a school District and the County Courts thereof were *exofficio* boards of school directors for their respective counties. They had the power 1st to divide the county into sub-districts—2nd to locate the school houses—3rd to levy and have collected when necessary the school tax for the purpose of building school houses under their supervision—4th they appointed the school trustees in the county—5th they appointed three persons as competent school examiners to examine teachers and give them certificates of recommendation—6th they required parents and guardians to send their wards to the public schools—7th they were to settle all difficulties arising in any of the schools of their county, remove teachers, and expel students, and make any separation of the students of the school, that might in their estimation be necessary to the harmony and success of the school—8th they made such by-laws, rules and regulations as they thought necessary for the government of the schools not inconsistent with the Constitution and laws. This was all well and proper, and would have worked well and satisfied the people. But this seems not to have suited the Governor, and he did not inaugurate the system under this law, but waited for the passage of the Act which he approved on the 24th April 1871.

By this last Act the salary of the superintendent is increased to three thousand dollars per annum. This superintendent who is himself appointed by the Governor, appoints for each judicial district of the State one Supervisor of education, who shall hold his office for four years unless sooner removed. His salary is five dollars per day. This Supervisor may be removed by the superintendent on the approval of the Governor. He divides the counties in his district into school districts, and has the power to appoint five school directors for each of his school districts; but in the exercise of this authority he is subject to the *supervisory control* of the superintendent. This supervisor is to enforce such rules and regulations as are adopted by the board of education. The superintendent of public instruction with the Governor and Attorney General are constituted this board of education for the state. They are made a legislative body with full powers to make laws and adopt all necessary rules and regulations for the *establishment* and promotion of public schools, subject to the Constitution and laws of this state. (It is well the Legislature put that in and I hope it may restrain the Governor.) The powers of this board are extraordinary. They provide for the examination and appointment of teachers and fix their compensation. They define the course of studies, and direct the class and kind of apparatus and books to be used; they prescribe the duties of the boards of directors, and generally, do all things not inconsistent with the constitution and laws of this State. The only limit to their power is that they prescribe no rule or regulation that will prevent the directors of the school districts from making any separation of the students that the peace and success of the school and the good of the whole, may require. Doubtless this Act suits the Governor and there can be no doubt that he wrote it and ordered it passed. In stockmen's phrase, "It has his mark and brand upon it."

By a little examination into this Act we will see that the Governor absolutely controls the entire school system. He appoints the superintendent, but we may be told that his appointment must be confirmed by the Senate, Yes, but when has the nomination of Governor Davis failed to carry *any man* through the Senate, or his recommendation failed to carry any measure through both houses? The school supervisors are appointed by this superintendent, with the approval of the Governor, and the superintendent Attorney General and the Governor constitute both branches of the legislature of this mis-called *Free* school system. The Attorney General also holds his office by appointment of the Governor. The Governor by this Act appoints and removes at least four thousand teachers in the State, and fixes their salaries. He appoints and removes thirty five supervisors who receive five dollars per day while employed. He, in *fact*, appoints one thousand school directors for the State. By this law the Governor exercises a power and influence over every child in the State, and moulds the minds of the youth, to suit himself. The child is taken from the control of the parent and placed under the control of the Governor of the State.

The Act approved November 6th 1871 makes it lawful to kill any one "in disguise who is engaged in any attempt by word, gesture, or otherwise to alarm some other person or persons and put them in bodily fear." The Legislature does not define what it takes to constitute disguise. A man who is in the habit of wearing a white hat, may be considered disguised if he is wearing a black one when he is slain. This Act is a slander upon the people of Texas, and is intended to produce the impression upon the minds of the people not acquainted with the facts, that there exists in Texas an organization known as the Ku Klux, and is intended to work upon the superstitions of the freedmen, and originate and put in action the animosity of the two races, and to secure to the administration party the support of those whose superstitions can be effected by such infamous legislation. This is plainly the object and intent of the act; and its effect will be to destroy the safeguards and protection which the law has thrown around the life of the citizen.

We will now refer to the act entitled "*An act further regulating proceedings in the several courts of the State of Texas.*"

By Sec I No person shall be excluded as a witness on account of color, *nor in any civil actions because he is a party to or interested in the issue tried.*

We object to this act for three reasons: 1st. It tends to multiply litigation. 2nd. It invites to fraud and perjury. 3rd. On account of the little credit found to be due to such testimony.

"Although, in the ordinary affairs of life, temptations to practice deceit and falsehood may be comparatively few, and therefore men may ordinarily be disposed to believe the statements of each other; yet, in judicial investigations the motives to prevent the truth and to perpetrate falsehood and fraud are so greatly multiplied, that if statements were received with the same undiscriminating freedom as in private life, the ends of justice could with far less certainty be attained. In private life, too, men can inquire and determine for themselves whom they will deal with and in whom they will confide; but the situation of judges and jurors renders it difficult if not impossible, in the narrow compass of a trial, to investigate witnesses; and from the very nature of judicial proceedings, and the necessity of preventing the multiplication of issues to be tried, it often may happen that the testimony of a witness, unworthy of credit, may receive as much consideration as that of one worthy of the fullest confidence. If no means were employed to exclude any contaminating influences from the fountains of justice, this evil would constantly occur. But the danger has always been felt, and always guarded against in all civilized countries. And while all evidence is open to the objection of the adverse party, before it is admitted, it has been found necessary to the ends of Justice that certain kinds of evidence should be uniformly excluded."

1st Gr. Ev. S. 326.

We will now examine the act entitled "*an act for the assessment and collection of Taxes approved August 5th* 1870.

By the 1st Section of this Act the Justices of the peace of the several counties of this state shall be assessors of taxes in their respective precincts under such rules and regulations as may be prescribed by law.

Section second of this Act declares that "a justice of the peace may be required to furnish a new bond, or additional securities *whenever* in the *opinion* of the District judge it may be deemed advisable. Should any justice of the peace fail to give a new bond and additional or other securities whenever required to do so by lawful authority, or shall appear to be delinquent in the performance of any important duty &c, he shall be removed by the district judge. This is in direct violation of section 24 of Article V of the Constitution which points out the only manner in which a justice of the peace may be removed, and that is " on conviction by a jury after indicment for malfeasance, nonfeasance, or misfeasance in office."

What advantage do the people gain by their right to elect their justices of the peace if they may be displaced from office at the pleasure of a district judge who is an appointee of the Governor?

This is a cunningly devised scheme to rob the people of their right of franchise. And this is not all. By section 7th, the Comptroller of Public Accounts shall communicate any instance of the misconduct or neglect of duty of any justice of the peace or any evidence of his incapacity furnished by *any thing* in the Comptroller's office, to the Clerk of the District court of the county wherein such justice of the peace was elected, which letter the Clerk shall lay before the court at the first term after it is received. The Justice is cited to appear, and if the District Judge shall consider there has been evident neglect of duty or misconduct in office by such justice of the peace, and if *he* shall be of opinion that such cause exists, shall make an order for his removal. Here we see that the Legislature has put it in the power of a district judge to remove at will any justice of the peace in his district, and has deprived the justice of the peace of his constitutional right of " *Trial by Jury.*"

Can any one fail to discover the object and intent of all this?

Whatever may have been the intent the fact is that District Judges do throw out honest men who are governed by honor, patriotism, and a sense of justice, in whom the people have confidence and in whose hands their rights and liberties are safe, and put in their stead such men as can be controlled for party purposes, and who will implicity obey the commands of those who made them. No man can accord a pure motive to a legislature that passes an act in itself harsh and oppressive and when the passing it, violates the plain letter of the Constitution which each member has sworn to support.

No man can be considered honorable or possessed of a pure motive who in order to gain an undue power over his neighbor's rights will stoop to moral perjury to accomplish it.

The cases are similar. In the one the Legislature has violated its oath of office in order to deprive the people of an important right secured to them by the Constitution. In the other, the man has sworn that he will do a certain thing for his neighbor in order to secure to himself a right belonging to his neighbor. Both are alike guilty of moral perjury.

The oath to support the Constitution is a promissory oath, and its violation does not constitute legal perjury, yet the oath is binding. All oaths are designed for the security of those who impose them. The people of Texas have imposed this constitutional oath on all the officers created by the Constitution. It is therefore manifest that this oath must be interpreted and performed in the sense in which the imposers intended it; otherwise, it affords no security to them. This is the meaning and reason of the rule "*jurare inanimum imponentis.*"

When the people declared through their Constitution that the justices of the peace might be removed from office on conviction by a jury after indicment, and the Governor and the members of the Legislature swore to support that declaration, how is it possible under any sort of strained construction that the Legislature could pass, and the Governor approve, an act giving to the District Judges power to remove Justices of the peace, before indictment found, and before conviction by a jury without a clear, palpable and willful violation of their oath of office.

We will now consider the act entitled *"an act to encourage Stock raising and for the protection of Stock raisers."*

The Stock interest of Texas is one of the most important interest of the State, and one which experience has shown requires the most stringent laws in order to effectually protect it from the encroachment of thieves and unprincipled men. We are therefore in favor of the passage of such laws as will most effectually protect the Stock raiser, and enable him to reap the benefit of his labor. This is due him from the State, he pays his taxes and helps to support the government, it therefore devolves upon the Government to render him secure in the possession and enjoyment of his property, without further expense or burden upon him. Does this law accomplish this end? We think not.

By section 1st of this act each organized County of the State not here in after excepted from the operation of this act shall be created an inspection district, for the inspection of hides and animals, and authorize the Governor to appoint in each district an inspector of hides and animals, who shall hold his office for four years. These officers are subject to removal at the will of the Governor. This section concentrates more power and patronage in the Executive.

By section 7th of this act "Every inspector or his deputy shall be allowed to charge at the rate of five cents for each and every hide or animal inspected over one hundred in number, and ten cents for each and all less than one hundred in number, which shall be paid by the person or persons for whom the inspection shall be made."

This creates a very heavy additional tax upon the Stock raisers. If the Stock raiser drives fifty beeves to his county town and sells them, he must pay the inspector of the district five dollars which is one per cent-um, if he sells his beeves at ten dollars per head. This is in addition to his regular advalorum State and County tax. This is not all, the inspector is to inspect all hides and animals sold in and taken from his county for sale or shipment "upon each of said hides he may charge ten cents, if less than one hundred in number. This is one percent-um more on each head of the fifty beeves which the stock raiser has sold, for of course this charge for inspecting the hides must ultimately come out of the pocket of the producer. This increases his tax to two dollars upon the hundred dollars worth of property, in addition to his annual direct advalorum State and County tax, and this is not all. By section 21st all animals intended to be driven or shipped to the Republic of Mexico, from any of the ports of Texas included within the counties, not excepted from the operation of this act, shall be inspected by the inspector of hides and animals at the point of shipment, or place where such animals are to be driven across the bounderies of the State, and said inspector shall be entitled to charge and collect for this service the sum of two and a half cents for each hide and animal inspected."

This also comes out of the Stock raiser in the end. This increases, this special tax to two dollars and twenty-five cents on every hundred dollars worth of property which he disposes of' in addition to his annual direct State and County tax.

Why should men who own this character of property be required to pay more than double the amount of taxes, required of men who own a different species of property. This act is violative of the 18th Section, Article 12th of the State Constitution, which declares that "Taxation shall be equal and uniform throughout the State. All property in the State shall be taxed in proportion to its value, to be ascertained as directed by law except such property as two thirds, of both houses of the Legislature may think proper to *exempt* from taxation. "If such a law as the above had been necessary to effectually protect the property of the Stock raiser, it was right and proper the Legislature should pass such, indeed it was their duty to do so, but the Legislature had no right to pass a law by which directly or indirectly the Stock raiser should be required to pay a greater amount in taxes than should persons owning a different kind of property. This act takes a very strange course *to protect stock raising.*

By section 9th of this act every Stock raiser is prohibited from buying a cow, calf, steer, hog, pig, sheep, or goat from his neighbor without the written authority of the person selling, which written authority shall not be deemed valid unless the certificate and seal of a district clerk or notary public is attached thereto; in order to get which in very many instances the party will have to ride twenty or thirty miles and pay the officer 50 cents for the certificate. There does not appear to be much encouragement to the Stock raiser in all this.

We have now reviewed the principal part of the general laws passed during the present administration, affecting materially the rights and liberties of the people, and in nearly every one which we have commented upon, we can see the hand of the Governor. His brain devised and originated them, we have been confirmed in this opinion from the spirit evinced in his inaugural address, and in all his messages to the Legislature, and by the frequent use of his pet phrases, which we find inserted in nearly every act. The most conspicuous of which are the following, "*a general supervisory authority over,*" "*Thoroughly subject to the authority of*" "*Under aud subject to the orders of*" "*Subject to the orders of the chief.*" The Governor uses one of these pet phrases, the first time he opens his mouth, to the people after his election.

In his inaugural address on the 28th of April 1870, he says, "while local self-government still remains, it is within the just bounds that there *is a supervisory power over all.*" The Governor does not define within what just bounds *this supervisory power over all* is prescribed. He next uses one of these phrases in his first message to the Legislature April 29th, 1870. Thus, "I recommend that a police system be adopted embracing the whole State under one head, and that the police of the different cities, the sheriffs and their deputies, and constables be made a part of that general police, to act in concert with it, and *to be subject to the orders of the Chief.*"

The act to establish a state police uses this language "all sheriffs and their deputies. constables, marshalls of cities and towns, and their deputies, and police of cities and towns, shall be considered part of the State Police, and *be subject to the supervisory control of the Governor and chief of state police.*" In the act to provide for the protection of the frontier we find this phrase. "Shall be given a *general supervising authority over.*"

In the act to provide for the Registration of voters, is this language. "*The Governor shall have Supervisory control over all registration.*" In the act to provide for the mode and manner of conducting elections &c, we have, "the *Governor shall have Supervisory control over all elections*, he shall have *control* over all *Sheriffs* and all other *police officers.*" The Governor's pet phrases are used in every law by which the Legislature confers upon him, or those directly under his control, some unconstitutional and unwarranted power, which abundantly prove, that the Governor not only furnished the Legislature with whatever substance the acts exhibit, but also the very language in which they were expressed.

We will here by recapitulation show the extent of the power which the Governor by his spirit of encroachment upon the other departments of the Government, has consolidated in himself, which creates, whatever the form of the government, a real despotism.

1st. The Governor declares quarantine on the coast of Texas, at will.

2nd. Appoints a physician as the health officer at each station.

3nd. He is authorized to raise and muster into service, twenty companies of Texas Rangers.

4th. He appoints the Captain of each company.

5th. He designates the ranking officer of each district.

6th. He has control and management of this entire force.

7th. He may disband the whole or any part of this force at will.

8th. He is commander-in-chief of all the military forces of the State.

9th. He appoints and commissions all general and field officers, company and staff officers, for the State Guard and Reserve Militia, and removes them at pleasure.

10th. He appoints one Adjutant General with the rank of colonel.

11th. He appoints a paymaster, whose salary is eight dollars per day.

12th. He organizes the Staff department and prescribes their duties.

13th. He designates the uniform to be worn by the State Guard and Reserve Militia.

14th. He appoints the officers to receive the fifteen dollars from all persons liable to serve in the reserve militia, who may avoid said service, by paying said amount, (which has been reduced by amendment to five dollars.)

15th. He may divide the State into military districts, and detail officers to command the same.

16th. He may order into active service the military forces of the State.

17th. He may place any county or counties under martial law, and suspend all the laws therein, until the legislature shall convene and take such action as it may deem necessary.

18th. He may levy a tax upon the people of the county or counties declared under martial law, to defray the expenses of the troops, &c.

19th. He designates the officers to collect this tax, and prescribes the mode and manner of its collection.

20th. He provides for the trial and punishment of citizens, in the counties in which he suspends the laws.

21st. He designates the officers for this purpose, and prescribes all necessary regulations for the formation and government of court-martials and military commissions for this purpose.

22d. He appoints, in each of the thirty-five judicial districts in this State, one District Attorney.

23d. He appoints for each of the one hundred and fifty-nine counties in this State, one County Treasurer, one County Surveyor, one Hide and Cattle Inspector, and all public weighers of cotton.

24th. He appoints in each county in this State, where a vacancy may exist, (and he may make a vacancy at pleasure) one Sheriff.

25th. He appoints a Mayor and Board of Aldermen, or officers of like character, for each incorporated city or town in this State, and also a Recorder for each of the cities of Houston and Galveston.

26th. He has "*supervisory control*" over all Sheriffs and their deputies, and police of cities and towns, and if they or either of them fail to obey his orders, "*promptly*," shall be removed from office.

27th. He has power at all times, in popria persona, to assume command of the whole or any part of the municipal police of any town or city, or of the Sheriffs, their deputies, constables, and marshals of cities or towns, and their deputies.

29th. He appoints a registrar for each organized county in the State, and may remove him at pleasure.

30th. He appoints a Board of Appeals and Revision in each organized county in the State, and removes them at will.

31st. He "*has supervisory control*" *over all registration.* We suppose this "*is within* (the Governor's) *just bounds.*"

32d. He (by and with the advice of the Senate), appoints a judge for each of the Criminal Courts of Houston and Galveston, and also a clerk for each of said Courts.

33d. He issues the bonds of the State of Texas, to the amount of seven hundred and fifty thousand ($750,000) dollars, for frontier protection.

34th. He is made the agent of the State to sell or dispose of said bonds.

35th. He is authorized to employ an agent or agents to sell the bonds, who shall be allowed a percentage not to exceed one per cent.

36th. He prints the said bonds, and the sum of two thousand dollars is appropriated for that purpose.

37th. He is to direct the expenditure of the seven hundred and fifty thousand ($750,000) dollars, appropriated by the Act of August 12th, 1870, for paying all expenses connected with the organization of ranger companies, on the frontier, and as to this matter the Comptroller of public accounts shall be *under the special direction* of the Governor.

38th. He designates thirty-five journals (newspapers) to perform and publish the county and judiciary printing and advertising of the judicial districts.

40th. He appoints (by and with the advice and consent of the Senate) a State Geologist, whose salary is three thousand dollars per annum and expenses paid.

41st. He procures rooms at the capitol of the State, for the deposit of the collections made by the State Geologist.

42d. He may cause to be sold, to the citizens of the State, the reports of the Geologist.

43d. He may remove the State Geologist from office and appoint his successor.

44th. He sells railroads indebted to the State, by deed of mortgage or other lien, and may if he deems it necessary buy in such road in the name of the State.

45th. He appoints (by and with the advice and consent of the Senate) a Superintendent of Public Instruction, whose annual salary is three thousand dollars. This Superintendent "shall have *supervisory control* of all the public free schools in this State."

46th. He (through this Superintendent) appoints for each judicial district of the State, one Supervisor of education who holds his office for four years, unless sooner removed by the Governor. It would seem that public instruction is one thing, and education another and a very different thing.

47th. He, with the Superintendent of Public Instruction and the Attorney General, constitute a Board of Education for the State.

48th. They adopt all rules and regulations for the establishment and promotion of public schools, and are empowered to levy and have taxes collected.

49th. They provide for examination and appointment of all teachers and fix their compensation.

50th. They define the course of studies and direct the class and kind of apparatus and books to be used.

51st. They prescribe the duties of the Boards of directors, and generally *do all things* they deem necessary.

52d. They prescribe the manner in which the school tax shall be collected and disbursed.

53d. The Governor appoints three judges of elections, to serve at each city or town election.

54th. He shall on the *days of election* have PERMANENT CHARGE AND CONTROL of the peace and order of the State over all peace and police officers. This means that the Governor may allow peace or not allow peace on the days of the election.

55th. He shall have "*supervisory control*" *over all* ELECTIONS. This means that the Governor shall or may control the elections to suit himself, which includes the power of declaring who shall and who shall not be elected by the people. If a county will go against *his* candidate, this we suppose authorizes him to tell his party to become *intimidated*, and not to go to the polls, and authorizes him to throw the vote out. It is time that such proceedings as these had ceased.

56th. He is authorized to employ an additional clerk at a salary of fifteen hundred dollars per annum.

We think this a good provision, judging from the many duties which the Governor is required to perform, one clerk in the Executive department is insufficient. It will occupy the time of one clerk to write out his martial law proclamations.

57th. He leases the penitentiary of the State.

58th. He appoints (by and with the advice and consent of the Senate) an inspector of the penitentiary.

50th. He hires the labor of the convicts of the penitentiary, (except such as are confined for murder.)

60th. He appoints three Commissioners to select a location for the Agricultural and Mechanical College of Texas, and also to build said college.

61st. He is authorized to advance the whole, or any part, of the five thousand dollars appropriated by Act of Legislature—for the release of children captured by the Indians—to such agent or agents as he may select, and may or may not require them to enter into bonds.

62d. He appoints a clerk to transcribe the charters of the towns of Reynosa, Comargo, Mier and Guerreo, in the Republic of Mexico.

63d. He procures the amount of money necessary to pay off all claims against the State, which the Auditorial Board may approve as valid, by the sale of six per cent. coupon bonds of the State, payable in twenty years.

64th. He is made the agent to sell these bonds and employ agents to sell them.

65th. He appoints any number of special policemen, not to exceed twenty in each county in the State, who receive three dollars per diem while on duty.

66th. He receives from the Secretary of the Treasury of the United States, all money due the State of Texas.

67th. He is authorized to have the General Index of Special Acts continued.

68th. He is specially authorized to issue commissions to Silas McCrary and Jerry Washington, as justices of the peace for Bowie county.

69th. He is authorized to have printed or engraved such an amount of bonds of the State, in value not to exceed four hundred thousand dollars, with coupons bearing ten per cent. per annum interest, to supply any deficiency in the revenue for the current and ensuing fiscal years, and for *other purposes.*

70th. He is authorized to sell these bonds at any price.

71st. All allowances of claims against the State under the Act approved May 22d, 1871, shall be *subject* to the Governor's approval before becoming valid claims,

72d. He, (by and with the advice and consent of the Senate,) appoints a Superintendent of Imigration, who shall be at the head of the Bureau of Imigration.

73d. He appoints through said Superintendent, four agents,

two for the United States and one for Great Britain and one for the Continent, and allows and fixes their compensation—not to exceed thirty-five hundred dollars each.

74th. He is authorized to accredit any number of traveling imigration lecturers, throughout the vast expanse of the terrestreal globe.

75th. He is authorized (" in case it should be deemed necessary, and should *so appear* to the *Governor*") to appoint one County Surveyor for two or more counties.

76th. He is authorized to instruct the Attorney General of the State, to take an appeal in a certain suit pending.

77th. He is authorized to suspend the sale of a certain railroad, advertised to be sold.

78th. He is authorized to make requisition on the Treasurer for one thousand two hundred dollars, to pay the costs of Court and expenses of counsel in the suit of John A. C. Grary, receiver, versus the Governor and Commissioner of the General Land Office.

79th. He " is authorized to invite Mr. Greeley to visit Austin, the Capitol, as the guest of the State. Said invitation to be expressed and conveyed in *such terms* and *manner* as the *Governor* may deem *befitting* the eminent character and distinguished public services of the honored guest."

In other words the legislature gives the Governor " a *supervisory control over*" the " terms and manner" of the invitation.

80th. He appoints (by and with the advice and consent of the Senate) the Judges of the Supreme Court, who hold their office for nine years.

81st. He is authorized to contract with any other corporation for continued construction of international railroad in case the company fail, at any time to construct the length of railroad as specified in its charter.

82d. He is authorized to fill by appointment, any vacancy in office of Mayor or Alderman of Jefferson city, prior to first Monday in May, 1872.

83d. He is authorized to receive, for the whole amount of principal and interest due this State by the Houston and Texas Central Railway Company sinking fund first mortgage gold interest bearing bonds of said company, the seven per cent. bond grant in exchange for the six, per cent. bonds of said railway Company, and of the Washington county Railroad Company, now held by the State for sums borrowed from the school fund.

84th. Coupons of State bonds to International Railroad Company, to be made payable at the city of New York, to such State agents as may be selected and appointed by the Governor, to pay the same.

85th. He is authorized to appoint a commissioner, resident in the county of Jefferson, to inspect and report upon the Sabine and Neches Rivers and Pine Island Bayou and Internal Improvement Company.

86th. He has control over the proceeds of tax levied to meet the payment of coupons and principal of State bonds issued to International Railroad Company.

87th. He is to sign and deliver to the president of the International Railroad Company, the State bonds to be issued.

88th. He appoints a Mayor, five Aldermen and a Constable for the town of Carthage.

89th. He appoints a Mayor and five Aldermen for the town of Rockfort.

90th. He appoints and removes all officers of the city of San Antonio, made elective, until the first general State election after August the 1st, 1870.

91st. He appoints one Mayor and five Aldermen, and one recorder for the city of Columbus.

92nd. He approves the appointment of Marshall for the city of Columbus.

We see from the foregoing that the Governor of the State has the power not only to fill such vacancies as casually occur, but is enabled by unconstitutional Legislative enactment to vacate nearly every office in the state at pleasure. The whole of the great power is concentrated in the Executive. The King of England is "The fountain of honor" The Governor of Texas is the source of patronage. He makes and unmakes directly or indirectly every officer in the government,

The intended check of the senate in the few instances in which its advice and consent are required by the constitution and laws has ceased to operate. The patronage of the Governor has penetrated the Legislative body, destroyed the capacity of resistance' and riveted it to the sweep of power, thereby enabling him to rule with more ease, and much more securely with, than without, the nominal check of the Senate. If the Governor has in the very infancy of our present government concentrated in his hands such an immense power and patronage, who can define the limit to the power he may assume to exercise, before the expiration of his term, and the result of the corrupting influence, growing out of and flowing from it. "Its influence over individuals will be multiplied to an indefinite extent; when the principle of public action will be open and owned, the Governor wants my vote and I want his patronage ; I will vote as he wishes and he will give me the office I wish for."

This is nothing more than the government of one man, and what is the government of one man but a monarchy?

"So long as offices were considered as public trusts, to be conferred on the honest, faithful, the capable, for the common good and not for the benefit or gain of the incumbent or his party; and so long as it was the practice of the government to continue in office those who faithfully performed their duties, its patronage, in point of fact, was limited to the mere power of nominating to accidental vacancies, or to newly created offices, and could of course, exercise but a moderate influence, either over the body of the community, or of the office holders themselves, but when this practice is reversed, (as it is in the present administration) when offices instead of being considered as public trusts to be conferred on the deserving, are regarded as spoils of victory, to be bestowed as rewards of partisan services, without respect to merit; when it is to be understood that all who hold office, hold by tenure of partisan zeal and party service, it is easy to see that the certain, direct, and inevitable tendency of such a state of things, is to convert the entire body of those in office into corrupt and supple instruments of power, and to raise up a host of hungry, greedy, and subservient partisans, ready for every service, however base and corrupt.

Were a premium offered for the best means of extending to the utmost the power of patronage; to destroy the love of country; and to subititute a spirit of subserviency and man worship; to encourage vice, and discourage virtue; and in a word to prefer one for the subversion of liberty and the establishment of despotism, no scheme more perfect could be devised; and such must be the tendency of the practice, with whatever intent adopted, or to whatever extent pursued."

We have no wish to diminish or to control, in any degree the constitutional authority of the executive office. We will here take the liberty of quoting largely from Mr. Webster, because what he has said upon the subject of the evil effects of excessive patronage, will have much more weight, than any thing we might or could say.

"The extent," says Mr. Webster, "of the patronage springing from this power of appointment and removal is so great, that it brings a dangerous mass of private and personal interests into operation in all great public elections and great questions, this is a mischief which has reached already, an alarming height. The principle of Republican governments, we are taught is public virtue, and whatever tends either to corrupt this principle, to debase it, or to weaken its force, tends in the same degree, to the final overthrow of such governments. Our representative systems suppose, that, in exercising the high right of suffrage the greatest of all political rights, and in forming opinions on great public measures, there will be a general prevalence of honest, intelligent judgment and manly independence, these presumptions lie at the foundation of all hope of maintaining governments entirely popular.

Whenever personal, individual, or selfish motives, influence the conduct of individuals on public questions, they affect the safety of the whole system. When these motives run deep and wide, and come in serious conflict, with higher power, and more patriotic purposes, they greatly endanger that system; and all will admit that if they become general and overwhelming so that all public principle is lost sight of, and every election becomes a mere scramble for office, the system inevitably must fall. Every wise man in and out of government, will endeavor, therefore, to promote the ascendency of public virtue, and public principle, and to restrain as far as practicable, in the actual operations of our institutions, the influence of selfish and private interests.

I concur with those who think that, looking to the present, and also looking to the future, and regarding all the probabilities that await us in reference to the character and qualities of those who may fill the executive chair, it is important to the stability of government and the welfare of the people, that there should be a check to the progress of official influence and patronage. The unlimited power to grant office, and to take it away, gives a command over the hopes and fears of a vast multitude of men. It is generally true, that he who controls another man's means of living, controls his will. Where there are favors to be granted, there are usually enough to solicit for them; and when favors once granted may be withdrawn at pleasure, there is little security for personal independence of character. The power of giving office thus affects the fears of all who are in, and the hopes of all who are out, those who are out endeavor to distinguish themselves by active political friendship, by warm personal devotion, by clamorous support of men in whose hands is the power of reward; while those who are *in* ordinarily take care that others shall not surpass them in such qualities or such conduct as are most likely to secure favor. They resolve not to be outdone in any of the works of partisanship. The consequence of all this is obvious. A competition ensues not of patriotic labors; not of rough and severe toils for the public good; not of manliness, independence and public spirit; but of complaisance, of indiscriminate support of executive measures, of pliant subserviency and gross adulation. All throng and rush together at the altar of man-worship; and then they offer sacrifices, and libations, till the thick fumes of their incence turn their own heads, and turn, also, the head of him who is the object of their idolatry.

The existence of parties in popular governments is not to be avoided; and if they are formed on constitutional questions, or in regard to great measures of public policy, and do not run to excessive length, it may be admitted that, on the whole, they do no great harm.

But the patronage of office, the power of bestowing place and emoluments, creates parties, not upon *any principle* or *any measure*, but upon the single ground of *personal interest*. Under the direct influence of this motive, they form round a leader, and they go for "the spoils of victory." And if the party chieftian becomes the national chieftian, he is still but too apt to consider all who have opposed him, as enemies to be punished, and all who have supported him, as friends to be rewarded. Blind devotion to party, and to the head of a party, thus takes place of the sentiment of generous patriotism and a high and exalted sense of public duty.

Let it not be said that the danger from executive patronage cannot be great, since the persons who hold office, constitute so small a portion of the whole people.

In the first place, it is to be remembered that patronage acts, not only on those who actually possess office, but on those also who expect it, or hope for it; and in the next place, office holders, by their very situation, their public station, their connection with the businees of individuals, their activity, their ability to help or to hurt according to their pleasure, their acquaintance with public affairs, and their zeal and devotion, exercise a degree of influence out of all proportion to their numbers.

We cannot disregard our own experience. We cannot shut our eyes to what is around us and upon us.

No candid man can deny that a *great* a *very great* change has taken place, within a few years, in the practice of executive government, which has produced a corresponding change in our political condition. No one can deny that office, of every kind, is now sought with extraordinary avidity, and that the condition well understood to be attached to every office, high or low, is indiscriminate support of the executive measures, and implicit obedience to executive will, (one almost imagines Mr. Webster to be speaking of the present administration, he pictures it so vividly.)

I am for arresting the future progress of this executive patronage. I am for staying the future *contagion of this plague.*

The theory of our institutions is plain; it is, that government is an agent created for the good of the people, and that every person in office is the agent and servant of the people. Offices are created not for the benefit of those who are to fill them, but for the public convenience; and they ought to be no more in number, nor should higher salaries be attached to them, than the public service requires. This is the theory.

But the difficulty in practice is, to prevent a direct reversal of all this; to prevent public offices from being considered as intended for the use and emolument of those who can obtain them. There is a headlong tendency to this, and it is necessary to restrain it by wise and effective legislation. There is still another, and perhaps a greatly more mischievous result, of extensive patronage in the hands of a single magistrate, and that is, that men in office have begun to think themselves mere agents and servants of the government. It is, in an especial manner, important to apply some corrective to this kind of feeling and opinion. It is necessary to bring back public officers to the conviction that they belong to the country, and not to *any administration*, nor to any *one man.*

The army is the army of the country, and is neither the mere instrument of the administration for the time being, nor of him who is at the *head of it.*

What is executive power? where does it originate? and how is it limited? We must go to the Constitution, where executive power is granted, defined and limited, in order to give a correct answer to these questions. The Constitution provides that "the executive department of the State shall consist of a chief magistrate, who shall be styled the Governor, a Lieutenant Governor, Secretary of State, Comptroller of public accounts, Treasurer, Commissioner of the General Land Office, Attorney General and Superintendent of Public Instruction, (to say the least we have a great many executives.)

The Governor may, by the Constitution, appoint the following officers, and he cannot appoint these except by and with the advice and consent of the Senate:

First, a Secretary of State.

Second, one Attorney General.

Third, Three Supreme Judges.

Fourth, a District Judge for each Judicial District in the State.

Fifth, a Superintendent of Public Instruction.

Sixth, a Superintendent of Imigration.

These are all the officers which the Governor can appoint. If this be true (and you can easily satisfy yourself upon the truth of it, by an examination of the Constitution) where does he get the power, which he has been so extensively exercising, of appointing to office every officer known to the Constitution and laws of the State. The Constitution nowhere gives him the power to remove any officer, yet he has been removing officers at pleasure—and without any apparent reason, other than a want of that perfect subserviency to his will, which he deems a disqualification for any office. Where does he get this power, seeing that it is not in the Constitution? He demanded it of *his* Legislature, and it of course passed an act giving him the power to make vacancies and fill them at pleasure. Nothing seems to be complete in the estimation of his Excellency, "without such powers are conferred on the Executive as will enable him in any emergency to act with authority of law." No power can be "conferred on the Executive," by the Legislature, which is not delegated to him by the people, and which is not prescribed and defined in their Constitution.

The Constitution also prescribes and limits the powers which the Legislative department of the government can exercise, and by no part of that instrument is the Legislature authorized to add to, take from, vary or change a single provision. The duty of the Legislature is to give effect to the provisions of the Constitution, which require Legislative action, according to their spirit and intent, and not to create powers or provisions which are not therein found.

By Sec. 14, Article 5, "all county and district officers, whose removals are not otherwise provided for, may be removed, on conviction by a jury, after indictment for malfeasance, nonfeasance or misfeasance in office."

The Constitution otherwise provides for the removal of the clerks of the Supreme and District Courts, by the Judge of said Court, for cause spread upon the minutes of said court. Constables may be removed by the county Court which appoints them, for cause spread upon the minutes of the Court. State officers may be removed by impeachment, and chief officers of the State by an address of two-thirds of the members elect to each House of the Legislature. Where, then we ask, does the Legislature get the power to authorize a district Judge to remove a justice of the peace? and where does the Governor get the power to remove a district attorney at will, as he has done in a number of instances in the last two years?

All the laws passed by the Legislature, authorizing the Governor to appoint officers, who are by the Constitution to be elected by the people, and to dismiss from office any *officer*, are unconstitutional, and declared by the Bill of Rights to be null and void. The Legislature did not pass such acts because they were constitutional, (for they knew they were *not*,) but because the Governor wrote them out and ordered them passed, or in other words, because he exercised his "*supervisory power over*" a majority of the members.

We will take occasion to say, that there were some men in the twelfth Legislature eminently patriotic, just and honorable, and of large experience, and whom the people will ever love to remember. But these few were so largely in the minority as to render them powerless in their noble efforts to keep the majority within constitutional bounds, or even within the bounds of common sense and humanity.

Their efforts to advise, restrain and curb the wild, reckless and destructive partisan passions of the heartless and brainless majority, proved ineffectual; it was love's labor lost. The situation of this small majority was pitiable indeed. They were compelled to stand by and witness the destruction of the people's dearest rights, to behold the Governor of the State, with his "*supervisory*" wand in hand, standing over the Legislature, and through them trampling upon and destroying the property, the liberty and the very life of the citizen, and they too powerless even to throw a stumbling block in the way of this unhallowed and destructive march. We know of no situation in life better calculated to render an honest, patriotic citizen miserable, than to have been a member of the twelfth Legislature of the State of Texas.

CHAPTER II.

The Oppressions of the Present Administration Exposed.

Under this head we purpose showing the manner in which the officers of the present administration, from the Governor down, have exercised the unconstitutional power vested in them by the Legislature of the State, and assumed the exercise of powers prohibited both by the Constitution and laws of the State. All candid men who carefully read and understand the laws must admit that the government under which we live, though in *form* a Republic, is in *truth* a Despotism, moderated only by the wisdom, the sobriety, and the magnanimity of the despot; and we will let the facts establish how moderate, how wise, how sober, and how magnanimous the despot has shown himself to be. The whole State is divided into military districts, and each district is placed under the command of an officer appointed by the Governor. The Governor is authorized to organize an army unlimited in number. He is enabled by what purports to be law, to supply this army, and to issue and sell the bonds of the State to provide the means for its support and maintainance. He holds the unsheathed sword and purse of the State, which are, to use his own language, "the recognized right arm of despotism."—Every civil officer in the State is subject to his "*supervisory control*," and made subordinate to this military establishment. If this is not despotism, history is false, and no such thing ever existed but in name. Webster defines despotism to be "absolute power; authority unlimited and uncontrolled by mere Constitution or laws, and depending alone on the will of the prince, as the despotism of a Turkish sultan." He defines a despot to be "an emperor, king, or prince, (names are nothing) invested with absolute power, or ruling without any control from men, constitution, or laws, hence *in a general sense a tyrant.*

Names, we say, amount to nothing. A man may become as great a despot under the name of Governor as under the name of king, emperor, prince or dictator. The force and effect is not in the *name*, but in the absolute power which the man who bears it wields and exercises. Constitutions amount to nothing where the power to enforce their provisions is assumed by the power which violates them, and where the power to violate them is recognized by the law-making power of the State. This is the power which the Governor demanded of and received from the Legislature. This is what he meant when he said "these measures will not be complete without such powers are conferred on the Executive as will enable him in any emergency to act with authority of law;" and in the same breath, "the question of making some provision for the temporary establishment of martial law, under certain contingencies and within limited districts, is therefore submitted."

The Governor by the laws appoints and removes, directly or indirectly, every civil officer in the State, controls the *order* and peace of the State, has absolute control over all elections in the State, decides who are to register and vote, prescribes the time when and the circumstances under which they may or may not vote, counts the votes or refuses to count them as his interests or inclinations may dictate, says how a citizen shall go to the polls, how long he shall remain at the polls, what he may or may not do while at the polls, says when he shall leave the polls, requires him as soon as he has deposited his vote to go straight home and "go to his usual employment." He has, since, at the head of this government, put in exercise all these powers by force of the bayonet; and if the people have murmured he has declared them insurrectionary and proclaimed martial law, established military commissions and extracted from them money, and in very many instances incarcerated them in loathesome prisons. If this be not despotism tell us what it takes to constitute it. And if the man who can do all this by " *authority* of law," and who has done all this, be not a despot, tell us what it takes to constitute one.

As we have given the law, we will produce the evidence. The Governor could not in person do all these things. He therefore must do much through his agents or tools. With this view before his mind he appointed only such men to office as were capable, willing and base enough to carry out his programme of oppressions. And it must be admitted that he has exercised a great degree of knowledge and discrimination in selecting these officers. A necessary element, therefore, in the qualification of his District Judges, was a total absence of consciencious honesty; for if they were honest, consciencious and just, the whole foundation upon which the Governor has based his oppressions would fall to the ground the very first time the question of the constitutionality of the laws, which confer these powers upon him, was properly brought before the Courts, which would nip his power in the bud, and destroy the foundation upon which his fulcrum rests—by means of which he expected and fully intended to prise from the people their constitutional, legal and even natural rights. The policy, practice and habit of the Governor is and has been to search any place, or seize any person or thing (by means of his State Guard and Police) without warrant and without probable cause supported by oath or affirmation. He contends that the uniform which the State Guard and Police wear, together with their silver badge of office, takes the place of the warrant to issue only upon probable cause, supported by oath or affirmation, and whoever bears about his person these badges of authority, may search any place, or seize upon any person or thing. We might give a number of instances which would prove the truth of this, but we will content ourselves by refering to one only; and we select the outrages inflicted upon the people of Hill county in December, 1870, by Governor Davis, through the medium of his State Guard and Police. On the 28th day of December, Lieutenant Prichett, at the head of three white and four negro police, all armed and equipped, appeared before James J. Gathings' residence, in Hill county. This party proceeded to surround and take possession of the house, alarming and terrifying the ladies and children in the house. Col. Gathings not knowing the men, and being aware of the fact that a man by the name of Jack Mitchell, who lived not far distant had been foully and brutally shot down in his night clothes, in his own house, in the presence of his wife, a short time before, protested against their entering his house, unless they produced some lawful authority for so doing. This they refused to do, and boldly said they had no authority and would have none, that their authority was vested in themselves by virtue of their position as police. The Lieutenant then ordered two of his negroes to cock their pistols and present them at Gathings; and while he was thus held in duress, the Lieutenant entered the house with the other five men and searched it, against the protest of Col. Gathings. After the Lieutenant had searched the house and premises and even the ladies' rooms to his heart's content, they left. Col. Gathings smarting under the outrages and insults offered to himself and family, felt it his duty to test by law whether such acts were proper and legal. He went to the nearest magistrate and made affidavit to the facts, upon which the magistrate issued his warrant for the arrest of the parties offending. This warrant was placed in A. M. Douglass' hands to be executed. He called on a few men to assist him in executing the warrant. He arrested the Lieutenant and party. When they had given up their arms, they were assured by A. M.

Douglas and Col. Gathings, that they would not be harmed, that their object was to have them examined before the proper civil officers. They were taken before the nearest magistrate, Justice Lawrence. Lieutenant Prichett said he feared he could not get justice before the magistrate at Covington, and desired to be examined before Justice Booth at Hillsboro. The change of venue was granted by the Justice, and the whole party was conveyed to Hillsboro, and their case was examined into by Justice Booth. The Lieutenant wanted time to procure witnesses and prepare his defence, which was granted him, by his entering into bonds, (for his appearance on the following Wednesday) in the sum of five hundred dollars. The privates of his party were discharged on account of some informality of the warrant. Proceedings were immediately instituted for correcting the informality in the warrant in order to re-arrest the privates, when they all including Lieutenant Prichett suddenly disappeared. When the day arrived on which the Lieutenant was to appear and answer the complaint of Col. Gathings, he made default. His case was called and his bond forfeited. We know Col. Gathings to be an honorable, honest, public spirited, high-toned and law abiding citizen. This is the very head and front of his offending. Let it be remembered also that Col. Gathings was charged with no offence and not even suspected of crime by those who placed him in arrest and searched his house. Lieut. Prichett and his State Police, in thus arresting Col. Gathings and searching his house, grossly violate the 7th section of Art. 1 of the Constitution which reads, "the people shall be secured in their *persons*, *houses*, papers and possessions from all unreasonable seizures or searches, and no warrant to search any *place* or to seize any person or thing shall issue without describing such place, person or thing as near as may be, nor without probable cause supported by oath or affirmation." This is very plain language, and needs nothing to explain it. "The people shall be *secured* in their persons." If the Governor can have the people arrested by any man or set of men who wear the uniform of the State Guard, without warrant, or color of authority, are the people secured in their persons? We think not. Was Col. Gathings secured in his person? The facts of the case answer the question. This section declares that the people shall be secured in their *houses*. If the Governor's State Guard can ride up to any man's house in Texas, assault the owner, put him under guard and search his *house* without warrant or any other legal authority, who will say that the people are secured in their houses?

"All *unreasonable* seizures or searches" are absolutely prohibited by this section; and all officers are prohibited from issuing a warrant to search any place, or to seize any person or thing, without the place, the person, or thing is described, as near as may be, nor without probable cause, which probable cause must be supported by oath or affirmation. The Legislature can pass no law by which this security of the people in their persons, houses, papers and possessions can be destroyed or abridged, nor can any power in the state assume to do it without becoming guilty of lawlessness and crime, and meriting the heaviest penalties. When these sacred rights secured by the Constitution are invaded what is the proper course for the citizens to pursue? The laws do, or ought to provide a speedy remedy for every wrong. The first step to be taken by the citizen when his rights have been invaded, is to lay his complaint before the officer provided by law; when this is done in legal form, it is the duty of the officer to issue his warrant for the arrest of the party or parties who have perpetrated the wrong, and examine into the facts of the case; and if the facts show that the law has been violated, by the parties charged, it is the officer's duty to punish the parties according to law. If he has not jurisdiction finally to try the case, it is his duty to bind the party or parties over to appear before the proper tribunal, and if an indictment or information be properly presented in the court having jurisdiction, it should try the case, and if the party or parties are adjudged guilty, to see that he or they suffer the penalty which the law affixes to the offence ; and it is the Governor's sworn duty to see that this is done, for the Constitution declares that "*he shall take care that the laws are executed.*" Col. Gathings pursued the course pointed out by the law. He filed his complaint under oath before the proper officer: the officer issued the warrant for the arrest of the parties who had violated the laws. A day was fixed for the trial; and Lieut. Prichett entered into bond to appear and answer the charges on a certain day; but instead of appearing he went to Austin, and reported the facts to his chief, (the Governor.) What was the sworn duty of the Governor under this state of facts? It was to execute the laws. This man was properly and legally arrested and bound in a bond to appear before the proper tribunal authorized by law to examine into the case. The Governor's only course under the law was to send him back to stand his examination. Did he do it? The facts will show. On the arrival of Lt. Prichett, a fugitive from justice, at the Capital, Gov. Davis summons before him his Adjutant or Chief of State Police, Gen. Davidson, placed under his command about eighty or a hundred State Guards, and ordered him to proceed with all speed to Hill County. Upon his arrival at the county seat, he sent his orderly and the sheriff of the county for Col. Gathings, Dr. Douglas and many other citizens, all of whom promptly obeyed the summons by making their appearance. They were carried to the Court House, from which all citizens were excluded and a heavy guard stationed around it. The prisoners were then informed by the Adjutant General that no military commission would be convened to try them if they would pay the expenses of the State Guard, which he estimated at five hundred dollars per diem. Col. Gathings protested against this course, declaring that he was innocent and had not violated the laws. The adjutant then informed him that he would declare the county under martial law, tax the county to support the troops, organize a court martial and try them, and if convicted send them immediately to the penitentiary, denying them appeal. Col. Gathings told the Adjutant he was not able to pay that amount. The Adjutant then informed him that $3,000 in currency would suffice. Col. Gathings raised the money among his friends and paid the $3,000. He with the others were then turned over to the civil authorities, and Col. Gathings was required to enter into bond in the sum of $2,000 and the others in the sum of $1,000 each. The Sheriff was required by the Adjutant to produce the bond which Lieutenant Prichett executed for his appearance before the magistrate to answer the the complaint of Col. Gathings.

From these facts, which are true, let the candid, unprejudiced reader decide who is guilty of a violation of the law, Gov. Davis and his State Guard, or Col. Gathings and the other citizens.—Let it be remembered too, that since this occurrence four Grand Juries have sat in Hill county and no indictment has been presented against Col. Gathings or any of the cittzins who were arrested by the Adjutant General and bound over to appear before the District Court of Hill county. This is a strong circumstance, showing their innocence, when we consider that the District Judges under existing laws, assume to themselves the right to select the grand and petit jurors. The Governor did not even suspend Lieutenant Prichett for his assault upon and illegal arrest of Col. Gathings, but sustained him, and made his illegal acts his own by ratifying them.

Who is this Lieutenant Prichett, and where is he? These questions we cannot answer. We only know that shortly after the Hill county affair we were accosted on the streets of Waco by an honest, hard working old freedman, who asked us to examine a paper which he handed us. We read it. It was an acknowledgement by Lieutenant Prichett of the receipt of seventy-five dollars, delivered him by the old man, with which he promised to purchase a mule for him, and if he failed to deliver the mule within a specified time he was to return the money. He told us he had called on Lieutenant Prichett for the mule or the money, and that Lieutenant Prichett informed him that he had bought the mule and had paid his seventy-five dollars for it, had loaned it to one of his State Guard and the fellow had run off with it, but he would catch him and deliver the mule; and that since he had this conversation with Lieutenant Prichett he too had mysteriously disappeared, and no one could tell him where he had gone. The old man seemed to be in deep distress. He said it was money he had saved from his hard earnings the year before to purchase a mule to cultivate a corn crop with. The name of the Sheriff of McLennan county was signed to this instrument as a witness. We speak whereof we know, and are responsible for what we say.

The State Guard is no other than a medium through which despotism is to pass without appearing to act directly from the Governor.

We will now see if his Excellency in the Hill county outrages has acted "*with authority of law.*" One would suppose that the militia bill was obnoxious enough for the Governor, and that there would be no necessity in violating it in order to wreak his vengeance upon the citizens; but not so. The 26th Section of this Act enables the Governor to declare martial law in any county at will, and to call out the State Guard or Reserve Militia to suppress any disorder; and prescribes that the expenses of maintaining the State Guard or Reserve Militia called into active service under this section may, in whole or in part, in the discretion of the Governor, be assessed upon the people of the county or counties where the laws are suspended. Did not the Governor disregard and grossly violate this section of his own Bill? How could the Governor under this section presume to try any citizen without a declaration of martial law? and how was it possible that he could assess the expenses of maintaining the State Guard, in whole or in part, upon the individual, Col. Gathings, instead of upon the people of the county? The only name for such an act is *oppressive Executive robbery.* It can be nothing less. Col. Gathings, up to the present, has failed in his efforts to get redress for these wrongs, outrages, insults, and oppressions. He would have instituted suit for damages against the Governor, in the Federal Court at Austin, but knowing the Governor to be execution proof, he desisted. He has no remedy at law under the present administration. If he fails in obtaining redress through the Courts of the country, through the influence of fraud, executive patronage and assumed power, what course is left him? None other than to fall back upon the law of nature; and all are constrained to believe that this is one of the objects the Governor had in view in perpetrating his oppressions, in order to force the people to open violence, so as to give his acts a color of necessity. The Governor by his violation of the Constitution and laws, and by his illegal proclamations, has made "the duty of man a wilderness of turnpike gates, through which he is to pass by tickets from one to the other."

Man's duty is plain and simple, and consists of two points: his duty to God which every man must feel; and with respect to his neighbor to do as he would be done by. If those to whom power is delegated do well, they willl be respected; if not, they will be despised. And with regard to those who assume powers which are not delegated, the rational world can only know them to hate them.

"No man entered into society to become worse than he was before, nor to have less rights than he had before, but to have those rights better secured and better protected. And his natural rights are the formation of all his civil rights. The natural rights of man are those which appertain to man in right of his existence. Of this kind are the right of self defence, self preservation, and the defence and preservation of those whom God has placed under *his* protection, his wife, his daughters, his sons; as well as the right of personal liberty and private property.

From what has been said three certain conclusions will follow:

"First. That every civil right grows out of a natural right, or in other words is a natural right exchanged.

Secondly. That civil power properly considered as such, is made up of the aggregate of that class of the natural rights of man which becomes defective in the individual in point of power, and answers not his purpose; but when collected to a focus, becomes competent to the purpose of every one.

Thirdly, That the power produced from the aggregate of natural rights, imperfect in power in the individual, *cannot be applied to invade* the natural rights which are retained in the individual and in which the power to execute is as perfect as the right itself."

The conclusion from the facts forces itself upon the mind that the natural rights which Col. Gathings has delegated to society for the purpose of better securing him in those rights have failed of their object, and have not only weakened that security and protection which were the sole motive in the transfer; but have in fact totally withdrawn that security and protection, by force of powers assumed by the Governor; not only so but the exercise of those natural rights which are inherent and inalienable has been violated and destroyed by force and fraud.

The Governor, by the course he pursued in Hill county has endeavored to destroy the unity and equality of man, which was recognized by God in creating him. "And God said, let us make man in our own image: in the image of God created he him; male and female created he them." No distinction is here pointed out but the distinction of sex. No other distinction is even implied.

In the future world, whether in Heaven or in hell the good and the bad are the only distinctions. The laws of all governments have been obliged to adopt this principle, by making degrees to consist in *crime*, and not in *persons*. But the Governor has altogether reversed this principle. He makes the distinction between *persons* and not crimes, for it was plain that Lt. Prichett was guilty of whatever crimes were committed in Hill Co.; but he being a State Guard "could do no wrong" and Col. Gathings, who was innocent, but opposed to the Governor in politics, and not being a State Guard, conld do no right, and for that reason was punished.

Are there any who regard themselves citizens of any state in these United States, who do not feel themselves interested in this matter? Is it no concern of yours that the citizens of Texas are oppressed and deprived of their property and liberty? that the sacred precincts of their homes are invaded by mobs of lawless men? that their fields are made desolate, and their dwellings draped in mourning? Is all this nothing to you? Have you no interest common with them in protecting and perpetuating the great and essential principles of liberty and free government and handing these priciples down to your children unimpaired? You cannot divest yourselves (if you would) of this unity of interest, any more than you can avoid the sudden and certain fate which will follow its violation, and if you attempt to divest yourselves of this unity

"*That fate is thine*—no distant date,
Stern Ruin's plowshare drives elate,
Full on thy bloom,
Till crushed beneath the furrow's weight,
Shall be thy doom."

The strong arm of the government, unchecked and uncontrolled by constitutions, laws or men will be turned loose upon your unprotected heads; and it will be poor consideration then, to know that all the other states are suffering the like oppressions.

This knowledge would be a poor recompense for the loss you have sustained and the pains you are forced to endure. Pause and reflect, and let reason resume her place!

"Is it nothing to you, all ye that pass by? behold and see if there be any sorrow like unto my sorrow which is done unto me." We have indeed fell among thieves, which have stripped us of our raiment and wounded us. Will you be like the certain priest, who chanced to pass that way, pass by on the other side? or like the Levite, look on us and pass by on the other side? or rather will you be like the good Samaritan, as you journey, come where we are, and bind up our wounds, pouring in oil and wine.

We will now show how the Governor has oppressed the people by usurping the power to make laws affecting their rights and liberties by proclamation.

In August, before the election for members of Congress in October, 1871, the Governor proclaimed that "all persons coming to vote shall deposit their votes with the *least possible delay*, and after this is done they are forbidden under any pretext to remain about the polls, or at the *county seat* (unless this is their residence) during the time of election, but shall return to their homes and *usual employment;* and peace officers, State Guard, or Militia on duty at the polls shall see that this regulation is complied with." This section of the Governor's proclamation is violative of Section 2, Article III, of the Constitution, which reads that "electors in *all cases* shall be privileged from arrest *during there attendance at* election and in going to and in returning from the same, except in case of *treason*, *felony* or *breach of the peace*." We think under this clause of the Constitution, an elector who lives in the country has a right to go to the polls at 9 o'clock in the morning, if it suits him, and has the right to wait until three o'clock in the evening before he deposits his vote, and if it suits his inclination he may remain at the county seat all night and all next day, and if he thinks proper to leave the county seat after depositing his ballot, he may or may not go home as his inclination, interest, or pleasure may dictate; and he may or may not, if he chooses to go home, return to his usual employment; he may arrange his toilet, get in his buggy and go to his neighbor's house and marry his neighbor's daughter, and spend a week with his friends; which would be novel and unusual employment for him. All or either of these things he might do and not be guilty of "*treason, felony* or *breach of the peace*," and by doing which he does not forfeit the protection secured to him by the organic law—the Governor's proclamation to the contrary notwithstanding. Any man, be he whom he may, who arrogates to himself the power to make and execute such a proclamation, in the very face of the Constitution he has sworn to support, is a *knave*, a *fool* or a *tyrant*. And the Governor, while he was canvassing the third Congressional District for W. T. Clark—candidate for Congress—said in his speeches that he would enforce this section of his proclamation, and if necessary would call out his State Guard, and if they were not sufficient he would call out his police, and if they were not sufficient he would call upon the United States troops to enable him to enforce it; and that Texas could not afford to loose the blood and treasure which resistance would cost." When I contemplate the natural dignitv of a man; when I feel (for nature has not been kind enough to me to blunt my feelings) for the honor and happiness of its character, I become irritated at the attempt to govern mankind by force and fraud, as if they were all knaves or fools, and can scarcely avoid disgust at those who are imposed upon."

We look in vain for a parallel case, except in the history of tyrants. "So James arrogated to himself the power of issuing proclamations, not merely to enforce, but to alter the law, not limiting this prerogative to any particular subject, and merely taking this distinction between a proclamation and an act of parliament, that the former is in force only during the life of the sovereign who issues it, whereas the latter is of perpetual legislation. He had accordingly issued (amongst others) proclamations against erecting any new buildings in or about London; and prohibited the making of starch from wheat. The legality of these coming in question, the Judges were summoned before the council with a view to obtain an opinion that they were binding on all the king's subjects. Coke at first evaded the question, expressed doubts, and wished to have further time to consider. The Lord Chancellor (Ellesmere) said that 'every precedent must have a first commencement, and that he would advise the judges to maintain the power and prerogatives of the king, and in cases in which there is no authority and precedent to leave it to the king to order it according to his wisdom and the good of his subjects, for otherwise the king would be no more than the Duke of Venice.' Coke answered, 'true it is that every precedent hath a commencement; but where authority and precedent are wanting there is need of great consideration before anything of novelty is established, and to provide that this is not against the law of the land; for the king cannot *change any part of the common law,* nor create *any offence* by his *proclamation*, which was *not* an offence *before*, without parliament.

* * * Indictments conclude *contra leges et statuta*, but I never heard an indictment conclude *contra regiam proclamationem*.'

Time was given and an unfavorable answer was returned, which saved us from the uncertainty which, to this day prevails in France, even under the Orleans dynasty, as to what may be done by royal *ordonnance*, and what can be done only by an act of the Legislature."—Campbell's Lives of the Chancellors, Vol. 2, pages 361-2. Our Penal Code is conclusive upon the point of the want of power in the Governor to create offences by proclamation, Article III, " In order that the penal law in force in this State may be *ample within itself*, and that no system of foreign laws, written or unwritten, may be appealed to, it is declared that no person shall be punished for *any act or omission* as a penal offence, unless the same is *expressly defined* and the penalty affixed by the written law of this State."

The 3rd section of the Governor's election proclamation reads, "all gatherings, combinations, or assembling of persons in numbers at or near the county seat during the time registration is being made or the election is going on, and for the purpose of intimidating voters is forbidden, and should any such gathering, combination, or assembly take place in any county *it shall be presumed* that the same is for *said purpose* of intimidating *voters* whatever might be alleged by such persons as the pretext thereof, and peace officers, State Guard, or militia on duty in such county are directed to disperse such persons; provided however, that in this regulation it is not intended to interfere with persons peaceably and quietly waiting at the registration office or at the polls for their turn to register and vote."

By this section of the proclamation the Governor has attempted to take from the citizen an important right and privilege secured to him by the constitution.

Art I, sec 19 of the Bill of Rights secures to the people the right, "in a peaceable manner to assemble together for their common good," and not only for the purpose of applying to those invested with powers of government for redress of grievances' but for any *other purposes.* And no executive officer has a right to alter or abridge this privilege, no assembling of the people, at any time or place can be prohibited by any power in the state while they conduct themselves "*in a peaceable manner.*" This right to peaceably assemble is a *privilege* secured by the Constitution, and the same instrument declares that "no citizen of this state shall be deprived of life, liberty, property or *privileges,* outlawed, exiled, or in any manner disfranchised, except by *due course of the law of the land.* This is a civil right, and not liable to be subordinated to the military authority.

This proclamation declares, "and should any gathering, combination or assembly take place in any county, it shall be *presumed* that the same is for said purpose of intimidating voters, whatever might be alleged by such persons as the pretext thereof; and peace officers, State Guard, and militia on duty in such county are directed to disperse such persons. Here the Governor violates that fundamental principle of the law which is as old as civilized society itself, the presumption of innocence, and our own code provides that "a defendant in a criminal cause is presumed to be innocent until his guilt is established by legal evidence." But how did the Governor propose to punish such as violated this section of the proclamation? By requiring peace officers State Guard and militia on duty, to disperse such persons. But suppose the people would not disperse; what then? Suppose the persons were arrested by the State Guard; before they could be punished or even called upon to answer, according to the provisions of our Constitution and the forms of our law, an indictment must be presented by a grand jury, or an information filed by the District Attorney in the proper court. Our Bill of Rights declares no persons shall be holden to answer for any criminal, charge but on indictment or information, except in cases arising in the land and naval forces, or offences against the laws regulating the militia," and this comes within neither of the exceptions. If these persons were prosecuted on indictment or information for a violation of this proclamation, the indictment or information would have to conclude "against the peace and dignity of the Governor's proclamation; whereas the law of Texas requires that all indictments or informations "*shall commence* 'In the name and by the authority of the State of Texas,' and "*must conclude*," against the peace and dignity of the State." Notwithstanding the Governor assumes "*a supervisory control*" over the laws and people of the State, he cannot destroy them or change the forms of these laws. The worst he can do is to harass, annoy and incommode the people by preventing them from enjoying the benefits and protection which they ought to derive from the laws.

What was the Governor's object and design in issuing this proclamation? Was it to secure to the people, all the people, a free, fair, and peaceable election? The facts prohibit such a conclusion; and his subsequent acts give the lie to such an intent. His first motive was to throw around the ballot box such an array of *peace officers, state guards, state police* and militia as to strike terror to the minds of all timid men, and thereby deter them from coming to the polls. The Governor reasoned in this way: there are very many honest, peaceable law-abiding citizens in the state who will say if they can't go to the polls and vote without being required to do it "*with the least possible delay* and if they cant stay at the polls or county seat after they have voted, but "*shall return to their homes and usual employment*," and if they are to be met at the Court House steps by a gang of State Guards, with loaded guns in their hands and pistols belted around their waists, and escorted and guarded to the ballot box as convicted felons are guarded to their cells in the penitentiary that they will not go at all. But we may be asked would this not deter the freedmen from coming to the polls to vote. The Governor was shrewd enough to provide against this contingency by obtaining from the Legislature the power to appoint twenty special policemen for each county, all of whom he, through his District Judges assigned to the duty of going all over their respective counties, and *forcing* the freedmen to the polls to vote. If this first section accomplished the object, all right; but if this failed to deter a sufficient number from voting to carry the election as the Governor wished, some other available means must be at hand by which the object could be accomplished. Some order must be proclaimed which we know the people cannot fail to violate, and if they do violate it in the slightest, our State Guard will be on the ground well armed and equipped, and if the emergency requires it, a riot or tumult can easily be gotten up, which will give some show of excuse forthrowing out the votes; and I think section 2nd of my proclamatlon will meet the case. Let me read it to you. "Section 2nd, All persons are forbidden to shout, jeer at, or in any way to insult or *annoy* voters or candidates during the registration or election, and peace officers, State Guard, and militia on duty, in any county where such *disturbance* may be attempted are directed at once to arrest such persons." I am sure, Mr. Newcomb, this will accomplish the end; for if any of these Texas boys should learn, while at the polls, that their condidate is ahead (and this is easily found out, as the two parties vote different colored tickets) they would be sure to break forth in a *shout* of joy and exultation, and then we could let slip the dogs of war; but this is not all. Did you notice that I use this language in the proclamation, "or in *any way* insult or *annoy* voters or *candidates* during the registration or election?" You know as well as myself that *nothing* can *annoy* a candidate more than to vote against him; and the annoyance increases in the same ratio with the votes cast against him, consequently whoever votes against our candidate, *annoys* our candidate, and our candidate is *the* candidate; whoever has annoyed the candidate violates this order, and the votes at that poll must be thrown out. You see the point?" "Yes; and a very fine point it is too!"

Proclamations can only have a binding force and effect when they are grounded upon and enforce the laws of the state.

Blackstone treats the subject of proclamations thus: From the same original of the King's being the fountain of justice, we may also deduce the prerogative of issuing proclamations which is vested in the King alone.

These proclamations have then a binding force, when (as Sir Edward Coke observes) they are grounded upon and enforce the laws of the realm. For though the making of laws is entirely a distinct part of the legislative branch of the sovereign power, yet the manner, time, and circumstances of putting these laws in execution must frequently be left to the discretion of the Executive Magistrate, and therefore his constitutions, or edicts concerning these points, which we call proclamations are binding upon the subject when they do not *either contradict* the old law, or *tend* to *establish* new ones; but only enforce the *execution* of such laws as are already in being * * * * "By the Statute 31, Hen. VIII, c. 8., it was enacted that the King's proclamation should have the force of acts of parliament; a Statute which was calculated to introduce the most *despotic tyranny*, and which must have proved fatal to the liberties of this Kingdom had it not been repealed in the minority of his successor." 1 Bl. Comm. 270. The Governor claims that his proclamation has the force and effect of law, and claims the power to enforce it as law, by force of the bayonet. This is "calculated to introduce the most despotic tyranny," and which must prove fatal to the liberties of the people if not checked.

In referring to the reign of Hen. VIII, Blackstone says, "It must be however remarked that (particularly in his latter years) the royal prerogative was then strained to a very tyrannical and oppressive height; and what was the worst circumstance, its encroachments were established by law, under the sanction of those pusillanimous parliaments, one of which, to its *eternal disgrace*, passed a statute whereby it was enacted that the King's proclamations should have the force of acts of parliament, and others concurred in the creation of that amazing heap of wild and new fangled treasons. 2 Bl. Comm. 4 31.

The Governor had still another object in view in issuing his election order. He desired to create the impression in the Northern mind that the people of Texas were a lawless set, and were disposed by force and intimidation to deprive the colored citizens of their right to vote. Whatever intimation of this kind is contained in his proclamation is totally unfounded and maliciously false and slanderous. The people of the North have been deceived by such false assertions and slanderous intimations long enough, and it is but justice to themselves and to us that they should examine into this matter for themselves and not be imposed upon longer. We invite a strict examination into our acts and conduct, our motives and our aims. The proclamation which we have been speaking of bears date August 9th, 1871. He issued another on September 6th, 1871.

In order that our readers may the better understand it we will insert it entire:

GOVERNOR'S OFFICE, September 6th, 1871.

" As a further precaution towards securing a fair, free and peaceable election at the canvass commencing on the third day of October next, the following instructions for carrying on the same are issued to the Registrar and judges of election in the several counties. 1. The registrar and judges of election are hereby instructed to report to the Governor all violations of the 'circular' issued by the Governor dated Aug. 9th, 1871, and providing regulations to the end that there may be no disturbance or intimidation at the registry of voters, and about the polls at the coming election. If any of the regulations or orders in that 'circular' are disregarded, or if the authorities and police or military appointed to enforce said 'circular' are prevented therefrom by lawless combinations too strong to be suppressed by the said authorities, the registrar and judges of election are instructed to report to the Governor and Secretary of State the number of voters who have been prevented from the free exercise of the right to vote, and the names of persons so prevented, as nearly as can be ascertained, also the names of the candidate or candidates for whom such person would *probably* have voted, had the election been allowed to be conducted in the manner required in said 'circular.'

"The registrar and judges of election are also instructed to report to the Governor the names of the persons who have violated the regulations provided in that 'circular,' so that such persons may be arrested and held for punishment under the laws of the United States and for this State, provided for the security of free elections.

2. As a further measure to secure fairness at the said election, the judges of election are directed previous to the opening of the polls to select one well-known and respectable citizen of each political party, who shall be permitted to be present in the room where the election is going on and remain during its entire progress, and during the counting of the votes. These citizens shall also be permitted to examine the seals placed on the ballot box at the close of each day, as provided by Section 23d, of the Act entitled "An Act to provide for the mode and manner of conducting elections, making returns and for the protection

and purity of the ballot box," approved August 15th, 1870; and also again to inspect the same when returned the following morning to the judges of election.

But further than as above specified, said citizens are not in any manner to be permitted to interfere in the election or in the matter of receiving and counting the ballots.

2. The attention of registrars is called to the Circular from the office of the Adjutant General, State of Texas, dated Aug. 1st, 1871, where it is provided that in case no officer of the State Police or special police is put in charge of the special police by order from Austin previous to the election, then the special police are to be under the "*supervision and order of the registrar.*" (Here is the Governor's own pet phrase again.) In such case the registrar is specially charged with enforcing the regulations of the above mentioned 'circular' of Aug. 9th, of the Governor. He will, if a sufficient number of special policemen have not been appointed, select others not to exceed twenty good men in all, who will be sworn to act as special policemen during the registration and election. The names of persons so selected will be sent to the Governor, with a statement of the number of days served by each. If an emergency should arise demanding a stronger force than is at hand of either State or special police, the registrar is authorized to call upon the nearest officer in command of State Guard (or of militia in the absence of State Guard) for detail of sufficient force to secure the enforcement of the regulations provided in said 'circular' from the Governor.

4. The Constitution having provided the secret ballot box* to secure perfect freedom in voting, any attempt to evade that provision by having a private ballot box apart from that estab-

---

*The Constitution nowhere provides for a secret ballot box, Article 12, Sec. 4, " In all elections by the people the vote shall be by ballot." This is the only provision.

lished by law, or any other device for the purpose of prying into the votes of citizens and by intimidation to prevent a free exercise of the right of suffrage, are forbidden and *must* be suppressed; and such private ballot box is to be suppressed; and such private ballot box is to be seized and destroyed, and the parties guilty of such attempt must be arrested, and held for punishment under the said law of this State, approved August 15th, 1870, and the Act of Congress of the United States for the enforcement of the fourteenth and fifteenth amendments, approved May 31st, 1870.

EDMUND J. DAVIS, Governor.

Strangers would conclude from reading this proclamation, or circular, that Texas was in a state of rebellion and insurrection, and that the Governor was in fact acting the part of a true patriot in endeavoring to restore order and peace; but this supposition is just the reverse of the truth. The Governor and members of his ring were the only men in the State who had raised the standard of rebellion and insurrection against the Constitution, the laws and the people of the State; but the people remained as peaceable, quiet and as obedient to the laws as ever any people did in any country.

The people, at a glance, saw through both these proclamations. They knew that the only hope for the Governor and his party was to obtain a pretext to throw out the votes, and that he had resorted to these flaming, unconstitutional, illegal, unwarranted, unnecessary and uncalled-for proclamations, as a pretext to enable him to accomplish his tyrannical purpose. Hence they determined not to violate a single section of either, however great the sacrifice; and when this was discovered by the Governor and his ring, John W. Oliver, judge of the 33d Judicial District of Texas, by the Governor's appointment, and a self-constituted leader of the Radical party in his district, attempted to inveigle the opposition into a violation of the Governor's *great election circular*, in order to carry out his nefarious purpose. He had telegraphed the Governor that his district would go Radical fifteen hundred majority, and he saw that something must be done or the truth would give the lie to his telegram. It was necessary, therefore, that something should be done, and done quickly. With this view, he called, through the columns of the War Register, the Governor's judicial organ for the 33d judicial district, a political meeting for the 19th of September, at the Court House in Marlin, Falls county, during the time registration was going on, and invited the Democrats to attend and discuss the political issues with them. When the day arrived he had the speakers' stand erected at the back door of the Court House. The Democrats not liking the course the straws took, politely declined participation, in a note to the Judge, assigning as their reason that the meeting was in violation of the 3d Section of the Governor's proclamation.

To this note the Judge returned a verbal message, saying that "if the Democrats were so tender-footed about the Governor's circular he would move the stand and assembly to the woods," which reply the Democrats received and replied in writing declining any participation, because even in the woods, the assembly would be in violation of the plain letter of section 3rd of the Governor's proclamation, "and should any such gathering, combination, or assembly take place in any county, it shall be *presumed* that the same is for the said purpose of intimidating voters."

He proceeded with the meeting at the door of the Court House while registration was going on, and the peace officers, State Guard or militia on duty in the county, did not obey their directions by dispersing such persons. The Judge was the chief of these peace officers, State Guard, and militia in his district, and not only violated the Governor's proclamation himself, but prevented them from performing their duty. About 3 o'clock in the evening a personal difficulty occured between two gentlemen, and a shot was discharged by one but no injury done. This created some stir among the freedmen, who flocked around the parties who had the difficulty. The Judge suddenly became as wild as a newly caught hyena. His hair stood erect on his neck, and in his wild leaps he landed through the window, into the Court House, through which he yelled to the freedmen to go and get their guns and return immediately. When the freedmen started for their guns, a worthy citizen of Marlin, walked up to Judge Oliver and calmly told him that if the negroes returned and one man was hurt, his (Oliver's) heart's blood should pay for it." The Judge instantly became as calm as a May morning; took the stand, and sent out runners in all directions with orders to tell the freedmen not to return with arms, and if they did he would put them in jail. The freedmen went home and large numbers of them armed themselves and started for town, but were stopped by the runners. The Judge and controller of the whole affair then made a speech, and told the people how he loved them, and what a good Confederate quartermaster he had been after he had worn himself out in the ranks and destroyed his health; but in the meantime he had closed the registration polls, and there were about two hundred citizens awaiting their turn to register, some of whom had been, in obedience to the Governor's Circular, peaceably and quietly waiting at the registration office for their turn to register, for three days—nearly all of whom were white men, the freedmen having already registered. Under this state of facts the citizens felt an interest in seeing the registration polls opened. Some of the citizens asked the Judge if the registration books would be opened the next day; to which he replied that registration was *closed*. Every thing now being quiet, five of the leading citizens waited on the Judge, and inquired of him what he intended to do. He answered that unless a sufficient number of citizens assured him that the law should be enforced, the county *should* be put under martial law. About thirty of the best citizens went to the Judge in the morning and delivered themselves as hostages, as a pledge of the peace and quiet of the county. His Honor accepted them and swore them in as special constables. (How a District Judge can make constables we can't see, but the Radical officers in Texas do anything they like.)

The Judge then sent these special constables out and had the two gentlemen arrested who had had the personal difficulty on the day previous, as well as about eight others. These parties were all bound over to keep the peace and for their appearance at the next term of the District Court. Before adjourning the Court, the Judge thanked the citizens for the prompt manner in which they came out for law and order, and ordered them to remain on duty until after the election. The Judge then went to his hotel, and Mr. Hart, the registrar, was asked when he would open the polls. He said he would not open them at all, as the Judge had no right to order them opened. The Judge was promptly informed of this. He went to the Court House and told the registrar that if he did not open the polls he would discharge him and place a man there that would. At the commencement of the trial of the parties who had the personal difficulty the day before, the one who brought on the attack (who was a member of the Radical party, notwithstanding which he is a brave and noble gentleman) rose, and in the spirit of his true manhood, took the blame upon himself, saying there would have been no difficulty, had it not been for him, that he had given the other party just ground for all he did. The other party, in every respect his peer, approached and extended him his hand, and they were friends.

The political meetings which Judge Oliver held at Marlin and elsewhere in his district, are the only instances of the violation of the Governor's Circular in the State, to our knowledge, and this you see was done by one of the Governor's own Judges; and we firmly believe that it was done with a design to get up a disturbance in order to control the vote at that box, or throw it out by fraudulent means; and that he was defeated in his design by the prudence of the citizens in not participating in the meeting and by the prompt and determined manner in which they met the attempt to rob them of their votes.

The Judge having signally failed in his attempt to intimidate the people of Falls county, and having failed to originate a "*contingency*" sufficient to justify a declaration of martial law, left Limestone county, where he had also called a political meeting, in violation of the Governor's Circular, breathing vengeance against the people of the District, and declaring publicly, in his political harrangues, that he was responsible for what he did and said to to no power but his God. But the people understanding his motive and seeing the cloven foot, by a wonderful degree of forethought and discretion, defeated his design again. He failed to get up a riot; but it was not long before an opportunity presented itself in Limestone county, which was seized upon by the Judge to prevent the freedmen from going to the polls during the election, by raising the cry of *intimidation, intimidation, intimidation!* The facts upon which this was based are these: On Saturday, September 30th, 1871, in Groesbeck, Limestone county, Mr. D. C. Applewhite was most brutally murdered by a squad of the Governor's colored State police. This victim of malice and misrule was well known as an auctioneer, at the terminus of the Texas Central Railroad, and was a gentleman of good standing and generally very quiet and peaceable, but not a man to quietly submit to gross outrages. The circumstances connected with his murder are these: He was standing in the drinking saloon of Zedick (the newly appointed mayor of Judge Oliver) conversing with a gentleman who had been previously arrested and released on bond. Applewhite made some remark that they would have a rough time arresting him without warrant. In a short time two policemen, armed, stepped up to them and said "*you are our prisoners.*" The gentlemen turned to face the policemen, when they (the policemen) commenced firing on them. Applewhite fled for protection in French's auction house, directly opposite, he being connected with the house. He was closely pursued by the police, who continued firing on him. He was compelled to leave this store and retreated towards J. C. Leonard & Co.'s bank, near which he fell—the policemen firing several shots into his prostrate and lifeless body. All the citizens who witnessed the affair were unarmed and could give the deceased no assistance. The policemen fled. Zedick, the mayor, called upon the citizens to arm themselves and organize, which they did; and numbers were mounted and ordered to go in pursuit and arrest the murderers. Two were arrested and lodged in the county jail at Springfield. The Reserve Militia organized to aid in restoring and keeping the peace. which was speedily effected, and everything became quiet. On the night of the day on which Applewhite was murdered, a freedman was shot and killed in Groesbeck, by whom, whether by a State police or a citizen is not known. Judge Oliver thought this was one of these "*certain contingencies*" referred to by the Governor when he *submitted the question* (to the Legislature) of "*making some provision for the temporary establishment of martial law within limited districts.*" Wherefore he proceeds as follows, to wit:

SPRINGFIELD, TEXAS, October 6th, 1871.

To his Excellency, E. J. Davis, Governor of the State of Texas —Dear Sir:—I have been here and have thoroughly, and to my entire satisfaction, investigated the conduct of the rioters of Limestone county, and to give you a detailed account of the outrages would keep me writing for a week. Suffice it to say, that I know of nothing in the history of the Government that so loudly calls and demands the most severe and summary punishment as the participants in this *hellish mob, hatred, malice, murder* and the complete and ruination of Republicans is the compound.

I can't do the subject justice, and will say that nothing less than the trial and punishment of at least fifty to one hundred men, by a determined Court Martial, backed by from two to three hundred brave and loyal men, will do any good; and unless this is done the whole matter will be a farce.

The rioters can prove anything they want to, and it is no use to prosecute in the Courts; and even if I were to arrest and try them, I would be compelled to try with jurors equally guilty as the accused, and it would simply be a foolish undertaking.

Now Governor, I am not excited at all, I mean precisely what I say.

I enclose you some statements of gentlemen, and I will say to you that some of the parties making the statements, tell me that they are afraid to tell the whole truth about this matter until they feel that this State is not to be handed over to the enemies of the Government.

I am going to stay with these scoundrels, and I commence on the morrow with some twenty or thirty of the ring-leaders; and I will do it or somebody will get badly hurt. Many of the villians are defiant, but I mean to test their grit before 12 M., to-morrow. Some of the villians are now getting very sorry, since I have created in their minds the certainty of the remedy to be applied to them. They say the good people want peace, and all that, but they always fail to say things that would protect anybody but themselves,

They see that it is going to cost something and they are sorry indeed.

Republicans must be protected, and an example must be made of this county, There are a few good men but they are afraid to offer resistance to the mob, which extends from one end of the county to the other.

Martial law and a Court composed of men of steel, and from two to three hundred troops, United States troops at that, if they can be had, is the only thing to conquer effectually these outlaws.

Telegraph to me, or write, as you prefer, what I am to expect.

I will say no more as I deem it unnecessary. I send this by Judge Imes, who is one of the Board of Appeals of this county, and who can give you his experience.

Yours, &c.,

[Signed.] J. W. OLIVER."

We might criticise the style and language of this letter, but will leave that to the readers, and only say that, it hardly reaches the standard of Lord Chesterfield in either.

It is not the production of a mind filled with charity—for "charity suffereth long and is kind; charity envieth not, charity vaunteth not itself; is not puffed up, doth not behave itself unseemly, seeketh not her own, is not easily provoked, thinketh no evil; *rejoiceth* not in *iniquity*, but *rejoiceth* in *truth*."

It is the offspring of a mind replete with envy, wrath and anger—"wrath is cruel, and anger is outrageous; but who is able to stand before envy."

Is his letter the production of a mind embued with truth; "let his own words condemn him," his own lips testify against him," "Now Governor I am not excited at all" Who can believe this and at the same time believe the writer sane. "And to give you a detailed account of the outrages would keep me writing for a week." If such a number of outrages had been committed in Limestone County as would have required a week's writing to detail them, might not this Judge, have given the Governor one instance, and if there had been one outrage perpetrated in Limestone County, other than those perpetrated by the State Police, *could* he have written this letter, without naming it, and giving the names of the persons who participated in it? If any body had been murdered, would he not have so stated—but all the murders had been committed by the police.

His letter does not contain a single instance of the violation of law, or resistance to lawful authority, by any man in Limestone County. What would this letter establish in a court of justice before a jury of twelve men; nothing against the people of Limestone County, but it would establish for its author, an unenviable character.

"The rioters can prove any thing they want to." Here he charges the people of Limestone County, directly, with subornation of perjury, he knew that this was not the truth. The people of Limestone County could prove, all that they wanted to, in order to vindicate themselves from the false and slanderous charges—and they did do this, by men of unimpeachable veracity.

"And it is no use to prosecute in the court." This implies that he could prosecute in the court, that the laws of the State were not obstructed, "and even if I were to arrest and try them" here he admits that he had the power to enforce the laws of the state in the county, by arresting and trying those, who have, or may violate the laws; then why the necessity of urging the Governor to declare Martial Law?

The 26th section of the Militia Bill, gives the Governor power to declare martial law, only when "the enforcement of the law of this State is obstructed, within any county, or counties, by combinations of lawless men too strong for the control of the civil authorities"—Judge Oliver further admits this fact when he says "I am going to stay with these scoundrels and I commence on the morrow with some twenty or thirty of the ring-leaders;" again, "They see that it is going to cost them something and they are *sorry indeed.*" If this clause in his letter be true, then we may even admit, all that it contains to be true, and then, upon his own showing, there was no necessity for martial law. The object of martial law is to put down such combinations of lawless men as are too strong for the control of the civil authorities, when it accomplishes this, it has performed its work. If these combinations of lawless men disband of their own accord, and become "*sorry indeed,*" that they did attempt to obstruct the laws, what necessity then remains for martial law. Judge Oliver's own letter proves conclusively that the enforcement of the laws in Limestone County was not obstructed—by any man or set of men, but by himself; and that the civil authorities could have arrested every man in the county, without resistance. "I would be compelled to try with jurors equally guilty as the accused, and it would simply be a foolish undertaking." Can this be true? where then were all the freedmen, and the white republicans. This Judge had been in the habit of selecting his own jurors; they were not drawn by the county court.

It was his habit, to order the sheriff to summon such men as he designated, to serve as Grand and Petit jurors, and his Sheriff was of his own appointing, he had a short time before, turned out the Sheriff whom the people had elected, and put in one of his own selecting; does he mean to say that there were not twelve men of the republican party, of both colors, in the county, who were not participants in this "Hellish mob, hatred, malice, murder, and the complete and ruination of Republicanism is the compound."

He well knew when he blurred the paper with this foul charge that there was not a single fact to warrant it. Every one who reads this letter must be convinced, that Judge Oliver's motive in having Limestone county put under martial law, was none other than to give the Governor a pretext to throw out the vote of the county, in order fraudulently to procure Wm. T. Clark a seat in Congress, and his letter establishes this fact. In one breath he tells the Governor " I would be compelled to try with jurors equally guilty as the accused," and in the next he says, " there are a few good men, but they are afraid to offer resistance to the mob which extends from one end of the county to the other." If this were true how could he " stay with these scoundrels," and how was it possible that he was going to " commence on the morrow with some twenty or thirty of the ringleaders," or "hurt somebody badly?" (The Judge's weapon is like that of Sampson, the jaw of an ass, with this distinction, in the one case, the ass was absent, in the other the ass was always present.) How was it possible he should do this, if he could not find twelve men for jurors who were not " equally guilty as the accused?" and if the few good men were " afraid to offer resistance," how could he expect them to commence on the revolters?

" I can't do the subject justice and will say that nothing less than the trial and punishment of at least fifty to one hundred men, by a determined court martial, backed by from two to three hundred brave and loyal men, will do any good," then these must be all who had violated the law—take his maximum one hundred, if one hundred must be punished, could he not find enough men for jurors in the county to try them? One thousand, one hundred and eighty-eight whites had voted at the election, and eight hundred and forty-three freedmen were registered in the county, which makes two thousand and thirty-one competent jurors, and yet the Judge says " I would be compelled to try with jurors equally guilty with the accused." Why did he not tell the Governor who were the accused, and why did he not accuse all those whom he refers to "as equally guilty as the accused?" This proves that his object was to have men punished and not crime. The sequel to the whole letter is this: "Republicans must be protected and an example made of this county." Must not the people of Limestone county be protected? No, Republicans alone, and all others must be made an example of—and such Republicans! "afraid to tell the whole truth about this matter, until they feel that this State is not to be handed over to the enemies of the Government." If this be true, the Republicans are not worthy to control the Government—and the Judge proposes to keep them in control, by having martial law declared and defeating the will of the people. Have not the people of Texas, at the proper time, through the ballot box, the right to determine into whose hands they will place the administration of this government. But it was impossible at that election, for the people to turn the government over to any one. They were not electing State, District or County officers. The election was ordered and held, to elect a member to the Congress of the United States. This ought not to have frightened the truth out of the Republicans. Truth is not so easily frightened. Was it not enough to slander the people of Limestone county? Must he add to this, the slander of *truth itself?* We will now examine what S. N. Jones and Mr. W. B. Bonner (Clerk of the District Court of Limestone county, by Judge Oliver's appointment and Registrar by the Governor's appointment) say in their statement to the Governor about the necessity for martial law. They say "in the name of God, Governor, help us, or we will be unable to maintain our positions as Republican." Mr. Jones, (the same man Judge Oliver refers to as Judge Jones,) was judge of election in Limestone county. Hear what these two intelligent officers say to the Governor of the State. They attempt to show the Governor that the Republicans on a fair election, had a majority of three (3) votes in the county. They say, "First, of the number voted, viz: 1188, at least seventy-nine had been objected to, by the Board of Revision, for good and sufficient reasons, and two hundred at least, had been improperly registered on a sixty days' residence in the county, instead of six months as the law requires, add to these say one hundred and fifty men, who were induced by the prevailing bitterness of partisan feeling, to vote against their inclinations, and we have four hundred and twenty-nine who are to be taken from those actually polled for the Democratic candidate. The entire number of the colored votes registered is eight hundred and forty-three, of whom fully two-thirds would have voted, and all have voted the Republican ticket. Deducting the rejected voters and those improperly registered, from the number actually polled, and deducting the number who would have voted for the Republican candidate, but who were forced by circumstances to vote against it, and adding them to the number who would have voted the Republican ticket, and we have a balance left to the Democratic nominee of seven hundred and thirty-four, and seven hundred and thirty-seven votes which would have been given to the Republican candidate, had a full, fair and impartial election been held."

This is a beautiful document to come from a Registrar and a Judge of election, and having passed under the eye of a District Judge, to be sent to the Governor of the State. Is it true? It shall speak for itself. "And two hundred at least had been improperly registered on a sixty days' residence in the county, instead of six months as the law requires." We don't know by what *law* this Registrar and this Judge of election were governed, but by the "act to provide for the registration of voters," passed by the Legislature of Texas, and approved by the Governor of Texas July 11th, 1870—to entitle a citizen to register and vote—it requires, "that he has resided one year in the State of

Texas and *sixty days* in the county wherein he offers to register." —Laws of 1870. page 34, chapter 16. This same provision is in the Constitution of the State in the identical language. Then is it true, as these men say, "that two hundred at least had been improperly registered." This is one of those statements of gentlemen which Judge Oliver enclosed to the Governor, and we suppose that these two men were some of the parties alluded to by Judge Oliver as being "afraid to tell the whole truth about this matter—it was well that something restrained them, if this was the character of their truths. The reader will see, that this little mistake of two hundred votes, will somewhat alter the result of the gentlemen's calculation. We will make the correction, and see how their report to the Governor would leave the vote of Limestone county. By their figures, the Democratic nominee had seven hundred and thirty-four lawful votes, and seven hundred and thirty seven votes which *would have* been given to the Republican candidate. Add these "two hundred at least," which they say were "improperly registered on a sixty days' residence in the county instead of six months, as the law requires," to the Democratic nominee, and it gives him a majority over the Republican nominee of just one hundred and ninety-seven votes. Did they wilfully misrepresent, with a view to impose upon the Governor, or were they ignorant of the Constitution and laws of the State? If the former the Governor should have displaced them instantly, as too base to hold any office; if the latter they should have been removed because they were too ignorant—and inexcusably so—to remain in office. This statement went through Judge Oliver to the Governor. He is a lawyer, or ought to be, and is inexcusable for sending up false statements, he cannot excuse himself by saying that he did not read it. How dare any man, claiming to be honest, send statements to the Governor, upon which he asks him to declare martial law in the county —suspend the writ of *habeas Corpus*, arrest, imprison and try the citizens—and force from them forty thousand dollars, without having thoroughly investigated each statement, in order to satisfy himself of the truth. If he knew it was false, he is more despicable than they who made it, and too infamous to hold any office of honor or trust, and should have been removed instantly for misfeasance in office. If he was ignorant of what it contained, he is equally criminal, and should have been instantly impeached and removed for misfeasance in office.

There is just about as much truth in the ballance of the statements which the Judge forwarded to the Governor—by Judge Jones whose experience the Governor is to receive, as is contained in this. The registrar, Bonner, and Judge Jones, the judge of election, perpetrates a fraud upon the other persons whom they induced to sign it by falsely representing its contents.

This is what the others say about it under oath. Hear them: Mr. M. A, Tucker says, "Now I have to say that I never saw or heard any such statement of the affair until I saw it in the journal aforesaid." The letter of Judge Oliver with all the statements, were demanded by the Legislature, of the Governor, after he declared martial law in Limestone and Freestone counties and were published in the State Journal, the organ of the administration on 13th Nov. 1871. Mr. Tucker further says, "that on Thursday the first day of the election, he furnished several freedmen on his place transportation to go to the polls to vote."

When they returned they informed him that they had not voted, that the bridge at Springfield was guarded, they were passed through by the guards and told that the way was open and all could go and vote." They went on into town and around the Square, but every thing was quiet and orderly, when they reached the square they were told by a colored man, that there was no use in their voting, that the election was not going on according to the Governor's order and that the vote of this county would not be worth any thing. They then asked my advice. I told them I would enquire into the matter for them, on Wednesday morning I addressed a letter to Mr. W. B. Bonner registrar of this county enquiring into the state of things at Springfield and in the evening by the hand of Charles Keillingen a mechanic, in my employ, I received the following note, from Mr. Bonner, which I have in my possession.

Springfield, Oct 4th.

Mr. A. Tucker

Dear Sir.

I decline to communicate to you in regard to validity of election, times are too pressing to trust any thing to letters or messengers unless I have implicit confidence in them. I would not advise you to bring any Clark men with you but we are anxious to see you, and wish you would come over immediately, Stevenson has finally withdrawn, every thing is working right for us.

Yours truly

(signed) W. B. Bonner.

I took no further notice of the matter until the last day of the election, when I went to Springfield. I arrived there about 11 o'clock A. M., remained about town until late in the evening, when I cast my vote just before polls were closed—I saw nothing during the day to cause the least intimidation, the guards treated every body politely, on Friday night after the vote had been counted I was requested by Mr. Bonner and others to sign a statement in regard to the election matter in this county; I enquired its nature and contents, which Mr. Bonner stated or pretended to state to me, I had confidence in his veracity and relying upon his representation of the contents of the documents I signed it. But his representation of the contents of the paper

I signed was very different in substance and spirit, from what I see published in the Journal.

(signed) M. A. Tucker, J. P.

Limestone Co., Precinct No. 2.

Witnesses, J. J. Lewis, A. C. L. Hill, R. A. Davis, W. G. Randall, S. J. Adams.

Mr. John H. Welsh, also makes affidavit, that there was no intimidation offered by Democrats, and further says. "That prominent Republicans did write and caused to be circulated through the county, certain letters urging the negroes that they must not come up and vote but stay away, and cry intimidation. That when the evidence was being compiled upon which the republicans expected to have martial law declared, one Sydney M. Jones, a manager of this election, asked me to sign the statement that was to go, and subsequently went, to the Executive of the State. I told him I could not sign it, for I considered the statement false, Jones then said, that he had pledged Judge Oliver that I was a good Radical and could be relied upon, and if I failed to sign it, it would go up to Austin by Bonner, and that Judge Oliver would doubt him, and he, the said Jones, would be in a bad plight with his party. He then said if I would sign said statement to save his character with his party, *he* would get to carry it to Austin ; that he and I would go to Rosse together and he (Jones) upon our arrival, would destroy the statement and after some days, report to Judge Oliver, he had lost it, and thereby it would never reach the Governor.

R. A. Clifton a Republican and a special policeman appointed by the Governor, makes affidavit to the following facts. "I will state further, that W. B. Bonner registrar, and S. P. Young sheriff of this county, told the negroes to circulate the report, and impression that there was danger, that by this means the election in this county could be "*thrown out*," so that the majority in the county for D. C. Giddings would be of no avail to the

Democrats. I will state further that some of the officers of the election, urged that all negroes whether of lawful age or not, be urged to register and vote, and the negroes offering for registration, should not be excluded by reason of minority; and that Sidney Jones a magistrate in Rosse precinct, gave instructions that all negroes, regardless of qualifications, should be brought to the polls and required to vote. I further state, it was agreed in *caucus* by the officers of the election, that every means that could be employed, should be, to throw out the vote of this county—and thereby destroy the large majority that otherwise would be given to Giddings. I further state that C. H. Newton, deputy-sheriff told me; he had sent word to the negroes, to stay away from the election, and further to arm for battle—C. H. Newton was also captain of the Police. I will further state that I was present when the following conversation, in substance ensued between Sheriff Young and Merrick Trammel, a colored officer of the police, to wit, Young stated to Trammel he had a warrant for the arrest of the negroes engaged in the killing of Applewhite, and asked if he would surrender them. To which' Trammel said, he would not. Young said are you afraid to go and vote. Trammel answered no. Young replied, Trammel you must not say that; you must say you are; its the only way we can get the vote of the county thrown out, and to carry the election for Clark,." I will state I intended to vote for Clark, the Republican candidate for Congress, and should have done so, but for the statement of Judge J. W. Oliver, to the effect, not to vote, as the Republicans intended to have the vote of this county thrown out.

(Signed) R. A CLIFTON, *Special Policeman.*

There are other statements to the same effect, but these suffise to show, who the "scoundrels' were, Judge Oliver told the Governor he was going to deal with. Was ever such villainy perpetrated, upon an honest people, by a set of officers—before the days of the present administration."

Jeffreys himself would have blushed at such vile frauds. Judge Oliver, in this matter is guilty "of violating the most solemn engagements into which man can enter with his fellow man, and of making institutions, of which it is desirable that the public should look with respect and confidence—instruments of frightful wrong and objects of general distrust." We did not expect any thing better from him, what Macaulay says of the traitor, Churchhill, applies with force to Judge Oliver, for men who have once engaged in a wicked and perilous enterprise, are no longer their own masters, and are often impelled, by a fatality which is part of their just punishment, to crimes such as they would at first have shuddered to contemplate."

How sadly true, and painfully applicable to Texas now, is the following page of history. "All those evil passions which it is the office of government to restrain, and which the best governments restrain but imperfectly, were on a sudden emancipated from control, avarice, licentiousness, revenge the hatred of sect to sect. On such occasions it will ever be found that the human vermin, which neglected by ministers of state and ministers of religion, barbarous in the midst of civilization, burrows among all physical and all moral pollution, in the cellars and garrets of great cities, will at once rise into a terrible importance." What the historian says of chancellor Perth, the apostate, is true of this man Oliver, "his nerves were weak, his spirit abject; and the only courage which he possessed was that evil courage which braves infamy, and which looks steadily on the torments of others."

This Judge will serve as an illustration of the Judiciary of the present administration, with here and there an exception, but these exceptiens are few, very few.

We will now give the reader some idea of this man, as judge upon the bench. He is uncouth, full of evil passion, vindictive, selfish, meriting nothing but contempt, therefore always suspecting he is held in contempt, by the bar and the people, never imposes fines, without adding insult to injury. We will give one instance. A young gentleman of exemplary character and deportment, entered the courthouse at Waco, during the session of the court. The court room is up stairs and is about forty feet square. The Judge's stand is against the wall at one side there is a railing running across the centre of the room, separating the Judge and Lawyers from the spectators. On the south side of the room and opposite the Judge's stand are two rooms, one used as the Clerk's office, the other as the Sheriff's office, the doors to each of these open on the steps leading down stairs. The gentleman went into the Sheriff's office, and when he came out, he did not take off his hat, he stepped from the Sheriff's office on the step and proceeded down stairs, after he was out of sight the Judge looked wildly around at the Sheriff and said, "follow that man just gone down the steps and bring him before the court." The Sheriff went in a run, and soon returned with the prisoner, when the following interesting dialogue took place.

Judge. "What is your name sir?"

The gentleman politely and modestly told him his name.

Judge. "Where do you live sir?"

Gentleman. "I live in Waco sir."

Judge. "What is your occupation?"

Gentleman. I am a professor sir, in the Waco university.

Judge, "What, a professor in a university, and got no better manners than to come into the presence of the court with your hat on sir. Now sir, if you had been some ignorant backwoodsman I might excuse you, but a professor in a university ought to have better sense, you will pay the clerk sir two dollars and a half and it will learn you better manners next time you come before the court." The gentleman attempted to explain, but he was balled at by his Honor. He proceeded to the clerk's desk, paid his two and a half dollars, and left the courthouse never again to enter it except on urgent business, while his Honor disgraces it. This is a fair illustration of the manner of assessing fines.

It would surprise the reader if he could see a list of the fines he has imposed at the different counties in his district (McLennon, Falls, and Limestone counties.)

We will now give an instance of his ruling on law points. He rules that, "words constitute an assault," and so charges his juries, Our code defines an assault to be, any attempt to commit a battery, or any threatening gesture showing in itself or by words accompanying it, an immediate intention, coupled with an ability to commit a battery." Art. 2137 Pascholis Dig.

The statute explains the terms "coupled with an ability to commit," thus Art. 2144. First that the person making the assault must be in such a position that, if not prevented, he may inflict a battery upon the person assailed."

2nd. That he must be within such distance of the person so assailed, as to make it within his power to commit the battery by the use of the means with which he attempts it." If his Honor's construction of the law be the correct one, this distance will depend in a great measure upon the state of the weather. On a cold, frosty morning a man might commit an assault at the distance of a mile, when on a cloudy and sultry day, he would have to be within one hundred yards or such a matter, of the person assailed.

This law argument of the Judge has not weight enough to keep one serious, the fault is less ours than his; and as we are willing to make an apology to the reader—for the liberty we have taken—we hope the Judge will make his for giving the cause. Our Code further declares, Article 2147, that "No verbal provocation justifies an assault and battery." Then it is evident, if words do not even *justify* they cannot *constitute* an assault. "No words will justify an assault."—Whar. Am. Cr. Law, page 463.

This Judge has an indictment now pending in his Court at Marlin, Falls county, in which a young man is charged with an aggravated assault, for talking roughly to some one while the party was in the house with the doors closed and locked, and the indictment charges the assailed party to have been in bed. I am not certain whether it charges the person assaulted to have been asleep or not. He has overruled a motion to quash this indictment.

This Judge has ruled, that a defendant convicted of crime in this State, has no right of appeal, by the Constitution and laws of this State; and in pursuance to this opinion, he sent two freedmen to the State penitentiary, denying them this right.

Upon this point our present Constitution reads, "In criminal causes no appeal shall be allowed to the Supreme Court, unless some judge thereof shall, upon inspecting a transcript of the record, believe that some error of law has been committed by the judge before whom the cause was tried; provided that said transcript of the record shall be presented, within sixty days from the date of the trial, under such rules and regulations as may be prescribed by the Legislature." The State Constitution of 1845 reads, "The Supreme Court shall have appellate jurisdiction only, which shall be coextensive with the limits of the State; but in criminal, and in cases of interlocutory judgments, with such exceptions and under such regulations as the Legislature shall make."

This clause has been construed, by the Supreme Court of the State, in the case of Saturner vs. the State, Chief Justice Hemphill delivering the opinion—than whom, no more profound and just judge ever graced the bench. "But in this State," says he, "the right of appeal flows from a higher source, it is guaranteed by the Constitution. It is true that the grant of appellate jurisdiction over criminal cases, is with such exceptions and under such regulations as the Legislature may make. Whatever may be the interpretation of these words, when they qualify other grants of authority, I cannot admit, that as usual here, they can be so considered as to make the right of appeal dependent wholly on the action of the Legislature. The rights exist under the Constitution; and had the Legislature failed to pass any law, regulating its exercise, it could not, if claimed, have been denied."—9 Texas Repts. 457.

Decisions of the Supreme Court have no effect upon his Honor, we have frequently heard him tell lawyers, who offered to read decisions applicable to the case being tried. "It is no use to read that decision sir, I have long since *overruled* it." In the two cases above referred to, the defendants were both sentenced by his Honor and sent immediately to the penitentiary. A motion for a new trial and in arrest of judgment were presented in proper form and within the time prescribed by the statute, both of which were overruled by his Honor; notice of appeal was given and entered of record, the statements of facts were agreed upon by the District Attorney and the counsel for the defendants, and approved by the Judge. The Judge refused to allow the defendants time to send a transcript of the record to a judge of the Supreme Court, and before the Clerk could find time to make out the transcript, this humane Judge had both the defendants inside the door of the State penitentiary. If this be not oppression, we know not what to call it!

In a short time (much within the sixty days allowed by the Constitution for forwarding the transcript) the transcript in each case was made out, and forwarded to Judge Ogden—one of the judges of the Supreme Court—and an appeal granted in both cases, and the following mandate returned to the District Court:

"THE STATE OF TEXAS,

To the District Court of McLennon County, Greeting:

Before the Hon. Paley Ogden, one of the judges of the Supreme Court of the State of Texas, in the case of the State of Texas, vs. Jackson Jenkins. The application of the defendant Jenkins for an allowance of an appeal, from the judgment of the District Court of McLennon county, was determined and therein, the said judge made his order in these words:

An appeal is allowed in the foregoing case, June 22d, 1871.

[Signed] PALEY OGDEN, Judge of the Sup. Court.

Wherefore we command you to observe the order of said judge in this behalf; witness the Hon. L. D. Evans, presiding judge of said Court, with the seal thereof annexed, at Austin, the 24th day of June, A. D., 1871.

{ L. S. } [Signed] W. P. DENORMANDIE, Clerk."

What was the District Court to obey? It was to suspend its sentence and let things remain *in Statu quo*, and retain the defendants in custody in the county jail, until the Supreme Court passed upon the case and affirmed or reversed the Decision of the District Court. But Judge Oliver had already passed sentence, and the Sheriff of the county had long before filed with the District Clerk of McLennon county, the receipt of the Superintendent of the penitentiary, for the bodies of these two men. The counsel for the defendants went to Judge Oliver and asked him to send to the penitentiary and get the defendants; he refused to do it, but said if the Supreme Court reversed the cases, he would get them out of the penitentiary by writ of Habeas Corpus. The counsel for the defendants immediately applied for the writ of *habeas corpus* in the case of Jackson Jenkins, which was granted by the Judge of the Supreme Court, the mandate ordering the Keeper or Superintendent of the penitentiary, to have the body of the applicant before him at the Supreme Court room, in Austin city, on the 16th day of September, 1871. The Superintendent made the following return upon the writ:

SEPTEMBER 9th, 1871.

James W. Talbot, Superintendent of the penitentiary, returns "that Jackson Jenkins was killed while at labor on the Houston and Great Northern Railroad, on the 27th day of June, 1871, while attempting to escape.

[Signed] J. W. TALBERT, Superintendent."

Is this not oppression? Is this not tyranny? The voice of that man's blood, to-day, crieth unto heaven for vengeance!

I care not if these defendants did not have the right of appeal by the Constitution, they did have the right to their sixty days to forward the transcript to the Supreme Court, which this Judge denied them, and in denying it he violated every principle of humanity and justice. Is this the sort of protection that the freedmen are to receive from the Courts of justice, under this administration? if so, the least that is administered the better.

We have heard this Judge charge grand juries, that the State Police and State Guard were empowered, and had the right and authority under the laws, to seize and hold in custody, any man, without warrant or other legal process, and that those political speakers who said they had not this right and authority, were *wicked and bad men*, and enemies to the government.

I can give the reader but a very imperfect idea of the Judge Nothing can give a correct idea of the man, but to see him, and witness his wild and insane ravings as he charges the grand and petit juries. On these occasions his eyes glare like a tiger's, he beats the cushion of his desk violently with his clenched fist, in fact he has become so frightfully terrible and self-important, that the goddess of justice has fled the temple and taken up her abode elsewhere; he has destroyed her emblems and broken her scales and given the fragments to the State Guard! Lord deliver us from such a scourge. We will give the reader one instance as an illustration of his rulings in civil cases: An attorney brought suit upon a simple note of hand, in the District Court of McLennon county. The note he had received from a firm of lawyers living in Lebannon, Tenn., with instructions to institute suit immediately and make the money. The suit was instituted, the payer being a citizen of McLennon county.

When the case was called the defendant by his attorney, read his plea in abatement to the effect that the plaintiff was not living at the date of the institution of the suit. The pltffs. counsel being satisfied from the evidence of the defendant's witnesses, that the plea could be sustained, dismissed the suit at plaintiff's costs. The Judge said that would not do, that he would enter up a judgment upon the minutes of the court against the plaintiff's counsel in person and by name for the costs of the suit. To this the counsel objected, saying he was not a party to the suit-but if his Honor thought that he wilfully brought the suit knowng at the time that the plaitiff was not in esse that he had the right to impose a fine for the contempt. The Judge said he knew it was not the fault of the attorney but the clerk and officers must be paid for their work "Enter up the judgment Mr. Clerk against the plaintiff's attorney" and it was entered up accordingly, and stands as a monument of his legal lore and justice on page 657 of the minutes of the District court of McLennon county, Texas. We have only a very few instances of the Judge's rulings on law points and they are such as come under our own personal observation. The people of the entire district, as well as all the members of the bar in the district having lost all confidence in Judge Oliver as a man and as a Judge, and being convinced that the fountain of justice could never be purified as long as he stood by to muddy its waters, presented him with the following petition, urging him to resign, which will explain itself.

"HON. J. W. OLIVER, SIR:—We hand you herewith, a communication from the members of the bar of the thirty-third Judicial District, soliciting you for reasons therein stated, to resign the Judgeship of said District. The unanimity evinced by this paper, we hope, will secure for it serious consideration, and produce in your mind the conviction deeply rooted in ours, that the best interest of the bar and people of the district, will be promoted and subserved by a compliance on your part with this request.

Very respectfully,

[Signed.] RICHARD COKE,
T. P. AYCOCK,
L. W. GOODRICH,
E. J. GURLEY,
B. B. CLARKSON,
Committee of Presentation.

The petition accompanying the letter, and handed to Judge Oliver in a body, reads as follows:

Hon. J. W. Oliver, Sir:—The members of the bar subscribing their names hereto, would respectfully represent, that events have occurred in the 33d Judicial District since your appointment to office, which have rendered you unpopular as a Judge and as a man, with the people of the District and with the members of the bar; that they no longer have in you the confidence necessary to be reposed in one in your position, and that this unpopularity and want of confidence is so universal, and so deeply felt, that the prospect of your future usefulness, as Judge in this district, is destroyed.

We have felt it our duty to inform you of these facts, and while painful, we believe it just to yourself, to ourselves, and to the people of the District, to say further, that your resignation would afford satisfaction to us, to them, and restore confidence in the administration of the laws through the Courts. We, therefore, present this as our petition to you, based upon the belief of the good results that would follow, requesting for these results, the sacrifice of your position by resigning it.

Very respectfully,

[Signed.] W. R. Reagan, B. B. Clarkson, B. F. Gassaway, Thos. Harrison, B. L. Aycock, Chas. A. Jennings, L. W. Goodrich, J. R. McDonald, J. D. Oltorf, E. J. Gurley, F. H. Sleeper, E. A. Jones, J. T. Dixon, Thos. Moore, Wm. L. Prather, E. H. Graham, George Clark, E. A. McKenney, W. M. Flournoy, J. F. Davis, L. C. Alexander, C. B. Pearre, W. B. Forde, Richard Coke, Thos. P. Aycock, S. C. Buck, B. W. Rimes, T. D. Williams, W. C. Smith, J. W. Speight, D. A. Kelley, J. M. Norris, G. B. Gerald, J. C. West, N. W. Ballte, John T. Flint, M. D. Herring, G. J. Buck, W. H. Jenkins, R. W. Davis, A. J. Evans, J. M. Anderson.

The following persons authorized their names to be signed, after the petition had been presented. Their names did not appear on the petition, at the time of its presentation, because the telegraph wires were down and they could not be communicated with. They compose the bar of Limestone county:

D. M. Pendergrast, L. J. Farrer, J. H. Smoot, Thos. J. Gibson, John A. Harrington, R. A. Davis.

The above compose the names of every lawyer in the District, of both political parties, except three, two of whom were in Polo Pinto county, several hundred miles distant, and the third was absent or not seen; all would have signed it had they been accessible.

One would suppose that the Judge would have yielded to this polite request of this great number of intelligent and high-toned lawyers. But not so. He was not prepared to give up such an office, as he had transformed the office of District Judge into, so easily. He immediately adjourned his Court (at Marlin) for several days, and ordered the Sherif, if he was not back on the day to which he had adjourned it, to call it and adjourn it from day to day until he arrived.

He went straightway to Austin to see the Governor, to caucus with him about the matter. He did not resign.

The Legislature, a day before they ádjourned, preferred charges of impeachment against him, and passed them, but before they had time to present them to the Senate that body had adjourned. Judge Oliver is now holding Court in Limestone county—the same he had put under martial law. How can he sit upon that bench of justice, which he had so disgraced, and look those people in the face whom he endeavored by fraud to destroy ?

We might record many other outrages and oppressions inflicted upon the people of his District, by the Judge of the present administration ; but these few instances will suffice to give an insight into his true character, and show the design of the Governor in appointing such to office. His letter had the effect he desired, and brought forth the following proclamation from the Governor :

"TO ALL WHOM THESE PRESENTS SHALL COME ;

Whereas, it has been officially made known to me, and the official reports have been corroborated by the verbal statements of individuals of good repute, personally cognizant of the facts by them stated, that there exists, in the counties of Limestone and Freestone, in said State, a combination of lawless men, claiming themselves to consist of several thousand persons, organized as an insurrectionary force too strong for the control of the civil authorities of said counties, which has murdered an unarmed and unoffending citizen, in his own house; the individuals composing which carry pistols and other weapons prohibited to be worn on the person by law; have discharged fire-arms in public places, and have by threats, violence and organized force, intimidated and controlled the civil officers of Limestone county, so as to prevent them from discharging their respective duties; who have precluded the holding a fair election in said last named county, and who even preseme to place picket guards upon the public highways, arrest and detain as prisoners citizens of the State, and stop the coaches carrying the United States mail, and interrogate, in an inquisitorial and menacing manner, the passengers therein; and to cut the telegraph wires to prevent communication with the seat of government; which insurrectionary force exists as an armed and organized body, contrary to law, and is too numerous to be arrested and held by the civil authorities, and to be tried by the District Courts;

Now, therefore, I, Edmun J. Davis, Governor of the State of Texas, by virtue of the authority in me vested by the Constitution and laws of said State, do hereby declare and proclaim martial law in said counties of Limestone and Freestone, and do order that the laws be suspended therein, and that the issuancy of the writ of *habeas corpus*, within or directed to said counties, or to either of them, be prohibited, until the Legislature now in session shall take such action as it may deem necessary, and until this proclamation is revoked; an assessment of fifty thousand dollars, or so much thereof as may be necessary, being hereby directed to be levied and collected off the property subject to taxation, of the resident citizens of said county of Limestone, where said combination organized, to be applied in accordance with Chapter twenty-two of the general laws of the Twelfth Legislature of the State of Texas, first session, 1871.

In testimony whereof, I have hereunto signed my name, and have caused the great seal of the State to be affixed, at the city of Austin, this 9th day of October, A. D., 1871, and of the independence of Texas, the thirty-sixth.

[Signed.] EDMUN J. DAVIS,
By the Governor. Governor.

JAMES P. NEWCOMB, Secretary of State."

The Governor by his proclamation based upon the false official reports, of his still falser officers, and the verbal statements of these worse than infamous individuals, shows no grounds for the declaration of martial law, in Freestone county. The 26 section of the militia bill from which the Governor claims to derive the power to declare martial law, only permits him to do it "whenever the enforcement of the laws of this state, is obstructed within any county or counties by combinations of lawless men too strong for the control of the civil authorities." He only charges that the civil authorities of Limestone county, were prevented from discharging their duties, and have by threats, violence and organized force, intimidated and controlled the civil officers of Limestone county so as to prevent *them* from discharging *their* respective duties." If there was no combination of lawless men too strong for the control of the civil authorities in Freestone county, and this is the only ground upon which the law permits the declaration of martial law; and the constitution of the state gives the Governor *no* power to declare it, did the Governor in *truth* declare martial law in Freestone county, by virtue of that authority in him vested by the constitution and laws of the State? No, it was the exercise of an assumed power, for the purpose of oppressing an innocent people and depriving them by force, of their property, as well as their right of franchise. Was it officially made known to him by Judge Oliver, that the enforcement of the laws was obstructed in Limestone county by any power too strong for the civil authorities. Not so but on the contrary he says: "I commence on the morrow to *arrest* some twenty or thirty of the ring leaders." and "they see it is going to cost something, and they are sorry indeed." If this be true does it not show that, even at the date of writing the letter and compiling the statements in order to get martial law declared, that whatever might have been the necessity for martial law in Limestone county prior to that date, that necessity had then ceased, and no longer existed. But not only so; does the Governor esteem the liberties, the property, the reputation, and happiness of the people of Texas so lightly, as to destroy them on official reports corroberated by verbal statements of individuals, without requiring both to be corroberated by the oath of the parties making them? What right has the Governor to hear verbal statements from any man, on a subject so deeply affecting the people as the subject of martial law, or no martial law. The very admission is a disgrace to any officer, holding the position he does. It shows a reckless want of care for the interests of the people.

Is it possible that the Governor has been criminal enough to put whole counties under martial law and imprison the citizens by hundreds, seize their property, and search their houses without probable cause, supported (not by verbal statements but) by *oath* or *affirmation*? The very constitution which he has sworn to support and from which he claims to derive his authority, declares "the people shall be secured in their persons, houses, papers, and possessions from all unreasonable seizures; or searches; and no warrant to search any place, or to seize any person or thing, shall issue, without describing such place, person or thing, as near as may be, *nor without* probable cause, *supported* by *oath or affirmation*." The official statement of Judge Oliver further shows that martial law was applied for, not because the enforcement of the laws of the State was obstructed by force, but because (to use his language) "the rioters can prove any thing they want to," for the argument we will admit this to be true. Does the constitution and the laws authorize any power in the state to declare martial law, because the character of the citizens for truth and veracity is suspected, or if you please is known to be bad. Show us the clause in the coustitution or laws which authorizes it. This is not assigned as a cause by either. But it is assigned by Judge Oliver as one of the reasons, why he did not choose to try the rioters, as he is pleased to call them, in the civil courts, and the only other reason he assigns for not trying them, is, that he would have to try them before jurors equally, guilty as the accused, neither, or both of these combined, constitute a basis for martial law, and the Governor knew it as well as he knew that there was not the shadow of necessity or cause for martial law in Limestone or Freestone counties, unless to elect a Democrat to represent them in the Congress of the United States, be a cause for the declaration of martial law. The Governor from the official reports and from the *verbal* statements of individuals, well knew the fact, and instead of carrying out the imperative injunction of the constitution "take *care* that the *laws* are *executed*," he had violated them for purposes so grievous that they cry to heaven. This is strong language but it is the language of facts.

Where did the Governor get the anthority to suspend the writ of *habèas corpus*, in Limestone and Freestone counties?

No such authority is vested in him by the constitution or laws of the State. Section 10 of the constitution declares, "the privilege of the writ of *habeas corpus* shall not be suspended except by act of the Legislature, in case of rebellion or invasion, when the public safety may require it." No power in the State can suspend the writ, except the Legislature, and it can only do it when one of the two conditions exist, in case of such a rebellion, as endangers the public safety, or in case of such an invasion, as endangers the public safety. Upon the evidence, before the Governor, the Legislature could not have suspended the writ. The Governor in his proclamation does not charge the people of Limestone and Freestone counties, or of either of them, with being in *rebellion* or in *invasion*, nor does he use any words of equivalent import; then if they have not been guilty of, and are not charged with being in that condition, which *alone* can subject them to the deprivation of the writ, how *could* the *Governor* declare these counties under martial law, even if the constitution had vested the power in him, under the state of facts, as he represents them to exist, in his proclamation. He says there was organized an insurrectionary force. The constitution authorizes him to call forth the militia of the State to *suppress insurrection.*"

It therefore follows, from the Governor's own showing, that the exercise of the power to suspend the writ of Habeas Corpus, in the two counties, was usurpation, and usurpation is *tyranny.*

Let it also be remembered, that by the Governor's proclamation of September 6th, 1871, he authorized the registrar "if an emergency should arise, demanding a stronger force than is at hand, of either State or Special police, to call upon the nearest officer in command of State Guard (or *militia* in the absence of State Guard) for detail of sufficient force, to secure the enforcements of the regulations provided in said 'circular' from the Governor." Said circular referred to his election proclamation of August 9th, 1871.

Those persons whom the Governor charges as a combination of lawless men, too strong for the civil authorities in Limestone county, and who carry pistols and other weapons prohibited to be worn on the person, by law, &c., were Captain Richardson's company of Reserve Militia, who had been called out by the registrar, in obedience to the Governor's proclamation, and were acting under the direction and carrying out the instructions of the Registrar, and preserving the peace of the county. So we see, as before remarked, that it was never intended that a militia force should be organized in the State, and the very first time that force is brought into requisition by the registrar, this circumstance is taken advantage of by the Governor and his officials, as a pretext to put the county under martial law. The sense of the Governor's proclamation was to leave out the militia entirely; for he encloses them in brackets, thus: ("or of militia, in the absence of State Guard)"

Foul deeds will rise,
Though all the earth o'erwhelm them, to men's eyes."

We might stop here, and the proof would be abundant to brand the Governor and his officials, with the basest frauds and oppressions; we will now show how guilty the people were pronounced by the court-martial appointed by his excellency. The 27th section of the Militia Bill reads: "Whenever the laws may be suspended, as provided for in the last preceding section, it shall be the duty of the Governor, to provide for the trial and punishment of offenders; and the Governor shall make all details of officers for this purpose, and prescribe all necessary regulations for the formation and government of courts-martial, and military commissions for this purpose."

He organized a court-martial, and in the language of his official, it was composed of men of "*steel*" but of that pure Demascus steel, keen enough to cut through, to lay bare, to dissect and totally destroy, and defeat their wicked and fraudulent attempt to oppress an innocent and unoffending people, and to deprive them of their civil and even natural rights, (so far as it was possible for any court-martial to do.) The members composing this court-martial discharged their duties like officers and men, as they were, "United States" officers at "that too."

They were men embued with the principles of common justice and humanity, they did not seek out *men* to punish, but *crime*, and the result was that not a man (in the "officials" language, "in this hellish mob, hatred, malice, murder, and the complete and ruination of Republicans is the compound") was declared guilty or punished. Then said this court-martial to all the people, we find no fault in these men, "for many bear false witness against them, but their witness agreed not together." When the Governor received the report of this court-martial, and the report of General Reynolds, and General Davidson, who had been there, and thoroughly, and to their "entire satisfaction, investigated the conduct of the rioters of Limestone county," and had before him, the "*detailed*" account of the outrages, .which would keep his "official" "writing for a week," and when he compared these with his "official reports, corroborated by the *verbal statements* of individuals of good repute, personally cognizant of the facts by them stated," what impression must they have produced on the mind of his Excellency, as to the character of those officials, and as to the repute of those individuals. He should have removed such of the officials from office as he could, and used his uttermost to have (such, as he had not the power to remove) the others impeached and removed. But instead, his official Oliver is still at large, and still acting as District Judge. His W. B. Bonner is still Registrar, and his official and individual, Justice of the Peace, Sydney A. Jones is still Judge of election. These three men sent up a report to the Governor, in which they accused the people of Limestone with insurrection, with intimidation of voters, with fraudulently registering, and voting, all of which the facts show, were falsely and fraudulently made. When the Governor received the report of the military commission, showing that there never did exist in Limestone and Freestone counties, any combination of lawless men, organized as an insurrectionary force, too strong for the control of the civil authorities of said counties, and that no man or set of men (but his officials) had precluded the holding a fair election in either of said counties, and that all the charges in his proclamation were based upon official reports, malicious and unfounded, and the corroboration of those reports were by verbal statements of men wholly unworthy of belief. What then becomes his duty as a christian, honorable, law-abiding Governor? He should have issued a proclamation revoking martial-law, and stated the true facts of the case as he knew them to exist. Did he do this? No! no!

On the 11th November 1871, he issued his proclamation in language similar to this. Whereas, order having been reestablished in Limestone and Freestone counties, and whereas the purposes for which martial-law was declared having been mainly attained: now therefore I Edmund J. Davis, Governor of the State of Texas, by virtue of the authority, in me vested by the constitution and laws of the State, do hereby declare the proclamation of the Governor of the State of Texas of date 9th October 1871, declaring martial-law in Limestone and Freestone counties revoked &c.

We will now point out the only "purposes" which were attained by the declaration of martial-law, in those two counties. The following official notice will show one of the objects attained.

"Office special agent State of Texas, Groesbeck, Limestone county, Texas.

Oct. 24th, 1871.

Pursuant to orders received from Major General A. G. Malloy commanding state forces in Limestone county, I am ordered to assess and levy a special military tax of Forty Thousand dollars ($40,000) to be paid by the citizens of Limestone county, to defray the expenses of military commission and State troops now on duty in said county.

I therefore levy a tax of three per cent on the hundred dollars of all taxable property situated in said county, as per assessment rolls of 1871.

All persons owning property in Limestone county are notified to appear at my office, in the city of Groesbeck, immediately, and pay the same, all persons refusing or failing to pay said tax within three (3) days from above date ten per cent, will be added, and their property levied upon and sold to satisfy said tax.

(signed) Geo. W. Farrow,

Special agent State of Texas, for Limestone county.

This, then, was one of the objects attained, no, only "mainly attained" for thirty-six thousand dollars ($36,000) instead of forty thousand ($40,000) dollars were collected from the citizens. The next "purpose attained" was the pretext by which the Governor threw out the votes of Limestone and Freestone counties. These were all the "purposes attained" under the Governor's proclamation of martial law. We suppose that if the assessment had been fifty thousand dollars, ($50,000) the amount designated in the Governor's proclamation, and the full amount had been collected from the people at the point of the bayonet, the Governor would have said in his proclamation revoking martial law, that the purposes had been *wholly* attained.

This is a fair inference from the facts. It is the only conclusion which can be derived from them. I have given all the purposes or objects which were attained:

1st. The collection of thirty-six thousand dollars from the citizens.

2d. A pretext for throwing out the votes of the two counties.

If this be true (and I refer the Governor to the reports of the military commission of General Reynolds and General Davidson, now on file in the Adjutant General's office, at Austin, for the truth of it) and the Governor in his revoking proclamation, says that the purposes for which martial law was declared "having been 'mainly attained,'" then the attaining of these purposes, which we show was attained, *must* have been the *purpose* for which the Governor placed the counties under martial law. We do hope, for civilization's sake, that the Governor, in his hours of calm reflection and pious meditation, derives no pleasure from the gratification of such purposes, such designs.

Can he expect the people of Texas to confide in, to revere or even respect him? He had as well expect the Ethiopian to change his skin, or the leopard his spots. Nor can he ever put himself in that condition which will merit the respect and esteem of the people, until he casts from him that ponderous load of official corruption by which he has surrounded himself, and breaks through that arch of fraud and oppression of which he now is the *key stone.* That arch extends all over the State of Texas, the material composing which are the Governor, the Secretary of State, the officers of the free school system, the district judges, many of the district attorneys, the Republican members of the Twelfth Legislature, the Sheriffs of counties and their deputies, the Mayors of cities and towns, the State and Special police and the State Guard, the Superintendent of Immigration and his sub-officers, and all appointees of the Governor; and these compose the great bulk of the white Republicans of the State, and all are under and "*subject to the supervisory control of the Governor.*"

This is the Grand State Arch, of which the Governor is the key-stone. There is a less arch, of which the District Judges are the key-stone; and still a lesser arch, of which the sheriffs are the key-stone. I exclude from this arch such appointees, and such members of the Republican party only as can look within, and who can, on a fair and honest examination, of their aims and motives, say with truth, and in the fear of God, "I *am honest*, and not in league with the oppressors of the people of Texas." We know a very few who can do this, and it is refreshing to meet them. They are like oases in the boundless desert.

We might refer to a number of the Governor's proclamations, declaring martial law, in various counties throughout the State, (for he has very many) but it would be a repetition of the like oppressions already detailed; and as our object is not to appeal to the passion, but the reason of the reader, we will desist.

The Governor has no difficulty, through his police and State Guard, in creating in any county or counties of the State, the "*certain contingency*," upon which he will declare martial law. They can create such a contingency, if there be a necessity for it, at any time and place, by killing one or more innocent citizens, as they did in Limestone county; and by so doing they run no risk of being punished in the courts—as they are now organized and conducted.

The Governor's originators of martial law contingencies, were it necessary, (if possible,) would originate a "*contingency*" in the very *Court of Heaven*.

We will now show the manner in which the Governor has taken advantage of his declarations of martial law, in depriving the people of their votes, and intend to deal fairly with him, but speak the plain truth fearlessly. We will here insert the certificate of election, which the Governor gave Wm. T. Clark:

"GOVERNOR'S OFFICE, AUSTIN, November 15th, 1871.

This is to certify, that on comparison of return of votes cast at an election held in the Third Congressional District of the State of Texas, on the 3d, 4th, 5th and 6th of October, A. D., 1871, I find that the Hon. Wm. T. Clark was duly elected to represent the said Congressional District of the State of Texas, in the Congress of the United States, for the term commencing on the 4th day of March, 1871, and ending on the 4th day of March, 1873.

In giving this certificate, I wish to call attention to the attached certified statement of the votes cast in the Third District as returned, with grounds for rejecting certain returns. This is explanatory of my reasons for giving the foregoing certificate of election. According to my opinion, the numerous irregularities and instances of fraud and violence, during the election in the Third District, reported and proved to my satisfaction, would rather warrant a new election than giving the certificate to either party. I have felt constrained, by my interpretation of the provisions of the State Constitution, on the subject of elections, to reject many returns, and would have thought it more just to regard the election as a nullity; yet the Act of Congress, of May 31st, 1870, Section 22, seems to require that I should give a certificate to one of the candidates.

In testimony whereof I have caused the great seal of the State to be affixed, at the city of Austin, the date herein above written.

[Signed.] EDMUN J. DAVIS,

By the Governor. Governor.

J. E. OLDRIGHT, Acting Secretary of State."

This certificate holds the Governor up, between the people and the sun, and enables them to look through him, and behold him as he is.

He says, first, in his certificate, that Wm. T. Clark "*was duly elected.*" Let us examine the import and meaning of this word "*duly.*" It means "properly; *fitly; regularly;* at the proper time."

Was Wm. T. Clark thus elected? Let the Governor's own words condemn him: "According to my opinion the numerous *irregularities*, and instances of *fraud* and violence, during the election in the Third District, as *reported* and *proved to my satisfaction*, would rather warrant a new election, than giving the certificate to either party. I have felt constrained, by my interpretation of the provisions of the State Constitution, on the subject of elections, to reject many returns, and would have thought it more just, to regard the election as a nullity." What have we here? A Governor of a State, giving a certificate of election to a party whom he himself admits, from evidence before him which satisfies his mind, that his election was irregular, fraudulent and accomplished by violence during the election; and he claims, that by his interpretation of the Constitution of this State, justice would have regarded "*the election as a nullity.*" And he perpetrates this self-admitted fraud, because "the Act of Congress, of May 31st, 1870, Section 22, *seems* to require him to give a certificate to one of the candidates. Let the reader ask the Governor if he did not help to make the State Constitution, and if he did not endeavor so to frame its provisions, as that they should conform to the Constitution of the United States. Ask him if the ratification of that Constitution by the Congress of the United States, is not proof positive that its provisions do conform to the Constitution of the United States. Then ask him if he has not taken the *double* oath to support both constitutions. How then could he be required to do an act which he himself admits, is violative of both constitutions under the pretext that an act of Congress "*seemed*" to require it of him If that act is violative of the Constitution of the United States, and if the Constitution of Texas is in conformity with the Constitution of the United States, then that act could have had no binding force upon the Governor. He admits that he knew that he was violating the Constitution and this act only "*seemed*" to require him to do it. But we will give the reader an opportunity to examine the said 22d Section of the Act of Congress, of May 31st, 1870, and let him judge for himself what it "*seemed*" to require the Governor to do; I will quote the whole Section just as it reads, and give him the full benefit of his cloak, which will prove to the Governor a Nestor's shirt. Here it is: Section 22, "And be it further enacted, that any officer of any election at which any representative or delegate in the Congress of the United States shall be voted for, whether such officer of election shall be appointed or created by or under any law or authority of the United States, or by or under any State, territorial, district, or municipal law or authority, who shall neglect or refuse to perform any duty, in regard to such election, required of him by any law of the United States, or of any State or Territory thereof; or violate any duty so imposed, or knowingly do any act thereby unauthorized, with intent to affect any such election, or the result thereof, or fraudulently make any false certificate of the result of such election in regard to such representative or delegate; or withhold, conceal, or destroy any certificate of record so required by law, respecting, concerning, or pertaining to the election of any such representative or delegate; or neglect or refuse to make and return the same as so required by law; or aid, counsel, procure, or advise any voter, person or officer to do any act, by this or any of the preceding sections, made a crime; or to omit to do any duty, the omission of which is by this or any other of said sections made a crime, or attempt to do so, shall be deemed guilty of a crime and shall be liable to prosecution and punishment therefor, as provided in the nineteenth section of this Act, for persons guilty of any of any of the crimes herein specified." This Section of the Act defines the offences, of any officer of election, and prescribes the punishment affixed to the offences described in Section nineteenth of this Act. How the Governor could have concluded that this Section *seemed* to require him to give a certificate to one of the candidates, we cannot devise. His office is not mentioned, nor does it prescribe any duty, he is, or is not to do, unless by implication it makes it his duty to see that his election officers, who managed the election and made the false returns, be punished as this Act prescribes, and we think this is plainly implied by said 22d Section. But instead of doing this, he stands charged with a violation of this very Section of the law, by indictment presented by the Grand Jury for the Western District of Texas. These Grand Jurors were all Republican save four. So the Governor is cut off completely from the cry of Rebels and party persecution. The honest men of his own party will not join him in his frauds upon the people, and have determined that law and justice shall once more reign in Texas, and that the people *shall* be secured in their right to vote. When that day arrives Texas will blossom like a rose. The people are now sad, on account of these oppressions, and on account of the false charges made against their loyalty to the Government, but this cry we hope will soon loose its charm The cry of "*the church*," "*the church*," "*the church is in danger*,' is what kept alive so long the tortures of the Spanish inquisition, and the fires of Smithfield were under the sacred name of *religion* ; hundreds and thousands of men, women and children were subjected to the torments of Hell itself. And in the name of Liberty the Governor has attempted to enslave the people of Texas, has deprived them of their property, and in very many instances thrown them into prisons and denied the rights secured to them by the Constitution, and his evident object is to turn the Government into a Despotism. Let it be remembered that there are only three sources from which governments have arisen, or ever will rise :

1st, superstition ; 2d, power ; 3d, the common interest of society and the common rights of man. The destruction of governments emanates from the very same sources and no others.

This Government is sought to be destroyed by a union of the two first, superstition and power.

When these two forces unite for the destruction of the Government, based upon the common interest of soceity, it is high time that freemen should look around them, and be fully prepared to throw themselves in the way of the march of this combined power, which brings in its train only chains and slavery.

We will now insert in full "the attached certified statement of the votes cast in the Third District, as returned," which the Governor appends to the certificate he gave to Wm. T. Clark. The Governor, when he rejected the votes of the various counties contained in this statement, well knew that it was wrong, unjust, wicked and fraudulent, and he had the evidence of this before him:

Statement of the number of votes cast in the Third district for condidates for Congress, at an election held therein, on the 3d, 4th, 5th and 6th of October, 1871:

COUNTIES.	W. T. CLARK.	D. C. GIDDINGS.	L. W. STEVENSON	REMARKS.
Austin	1,322	1,348	6	
Bosque	77	457	....	Rejected. No official returns were received
Brazoria	850	386	30	
Brazos	1,050	1,233	....	Rejected. The tickets were marked with numbers, contrary to provisions of section 19, chapter 78, general laws, fall session 12th Legislature, 1870, thereby operating as a scrutiny upon the votes and a restraint upon the freedom of voters. Further, that 49 of foreign birth, had been permitted to register and vote without legal proof of naturalization.
Burleson	478	829	....	
Falls	960	931	2	
Fort Bend	1,207	345	....	Rejected. Acts of violence and intimida-
Freestone	780	1,147	....	tion and armed disturbance have been shown to have materially interfered with the purity and freedom of the election, thereby preventing such a number of the qualified electors therein from voting, as would have changed the result of the election in that county, if they had been permitted freely to vote. Further, among those who voted at that election, 163 persons had been permitted to register by proxy, contrary to law.

Galveston ...	304	1,693	329	
Grimes	1,698	1,293	....	
Harris.	2,033	1,621	....	Six hundred and twenty-one voters reported as having been deterred from voting for W. T. Clark, as desired by them, not counted, because though those names appear on registration list and though it is likely that some or all of them desired to vote as alleged, it is considered that under the act of Congress, the application must come from the voters themselves, and this they have not made.
Hill............	455	649	....	
Leon..........	598	1,027	1	
Limestone...	28	1,153	1	Rejected. Reasons same as for Freestone, except as regards the 163 votes.
Madison.....	161	429	....	
Matagorda...	304	151	3	
McLennon...	1,162	1,520	....	
Milam.........	299	976	....	
Montgomery	543	596	....	
Navarro......	981	1,000	....	
Rotertson....	1,144	1,373	13	
Walker.......	848	720	18	The votes received at the "White Man's" place of voting, at what was called "the white man's ballot boxes," are rejected, because two voting places are not allowed by law, and because that box was not presided over by even one lawful officer. Also because 458 aliens were registered on declaration of intention to become citizens, made by them in vacation, before a clerk, and not in term time, before a competent Court, of whom or nearly all voted at what was called "the white man's box," and for other sufficient causes. The votes cast at the lawful box are alone counted.
Washington	2,535	110	....	
Wharton.....	525	85	7	
Total.......	18,407	17,082	408	

DEPARTMENT OF STATE,
AUSTIN, November 14th, 1871.

J. E. Oldright, Acting Secretary of State, for the State of Texas, hereby certifies that the foregoing is a true copy, taken from the records of this office, witness my hand and official seal, at office in city of Austin, the date above written.

J. E. OLDRIGHT,
Acting Secretary of State.

This thing, for I know not what to call it, was the very thing the Governor had in his mind, when he wrote out, or had written out the act entitled "an act to provide for the mode and manner of conducting elections, making returns, and for the protection and purity of the ballot-box," approved August 15th, 1870. Section 58, "the Governor shall have "*supervisory control over all electi ons*,, * * * * * "To this and he shall have control over all sheriffs and all other peace-officers. who shall obey his orders &c.

Again sect. 52, "on the days of election he (the Governor) shall have paramount charge and control of the peace and order of the State, over all peace and police officers, and shall have the command and direction *in* chief of all police officers by whomsoever appointed, and of all sheriffs and constables in their capacity of officers of the peace."

We will now review the Governor's attached statement. He puts Bosque county down seventy seven for Clark, and four hundred and fifty seven for D. C. Giddings, opposite to these figures he puts "rejected—No official returns were received."

Then what did the Governor reject? and where did the Governor get his figures?
If the vote was not officially returned it was his duty to have it officially returned, by the proper returning officer, else why the necessity of giving him a "*supervisory control*" over all elections."

Did the Governor take the "verbal statements of gentlemen of good repute, personally cognizant of the facts by them stated? and upon this, throw out the vote of Bosque county. This is a "*supervisory control*" over elections with a vengeance. Why was the vote not returned? He throws out the vote of Bosque county, because, "the tickets were marked with numbers contrary to provisions of section 19 chapter 78, General Laws, Fall session, 12th Legislature 1870."

We will now see what power that section gives the Governor

to reject votes, because they are marked. We will quote this section for the Governor's information, and future guidence, and we hope he will read it. Sect. 19. "That upon the ticket of each voter having the right to vote for only a *portion* of the officers to be elected at any election, one of the Judges of election shall write one or all the words "State" "District" and "Congress" according as the voter of such ticket shall have the right to vote for state and district officers, and members of congress, or a portion of the same; and the name or names of no candidates, for any office or offices, other than those indicated by the word or words written by the Judge of election on the ticket, shall be considered or counted by the Judges of election. and any Judge of election placing upon any ticket, any other word or mark than that herein provided for, shall be deemed guilty of a misdemeanor, and upon conviction thereof, shall be fined not less than one hundred dollars, nor more than five hundred dollars." We see nothing in this language to authorize the Governor to reject and refuse to count the votes of any county, for the reason he assigns, or for, any reason he could or might assign; nor does it authorize the Judges of election, to refuse to count the votes, because the tickets are marked with numbers, nor because they have any other marks upon them. They may refuse to consider or count, only, the votes for such candidates, whose names may be placed on the tickets by the voters, which are not designated by the words, "State" "District" and "Congress" or one or more of them, placed on the ticket, by one of the Judges of election. To illustrate, A's residence is Limestone county on the day of the election he is in Brazos county, Limestone and Brazos counties being in the same congressional district, he may under the constitution and laws of the State of Texas, vote for the candidate for congress in either, or in any county in the district. He hands his ticket to the Judge of election, and the Judge writes across the back of it "congress." But when the

Judges of election open this ticket and find that he has not only voted for D. C. Giddings, candidate for congress in the 3rd District, but has also voted for B, for district attorney, and Limestone county not being in the same Judicial District with Brazos.

This 19th section makes it the duty of the Judges, to consider and count his vote for the member of congress, because it is a legal vote, and to refuse to consider or count his vote for district attorney, because it is an illegal vote, and it makes no difference whether the illegal vote cast for the district attorney, was the result of inadvertence, or mistake, or fraud, for "the name or names of no *candidate* or *candidates* for any office or offices, *other than* those indicated by the word or words, written by the Judge of election, on the ticket shall be considered or counted by the Judges, of election," "and it must follow as the night the day" that the name or names of the candidate or candidates for any office or offices, *indicated* by the word or words written by the Judge of election on the ticket, *shall be considered, and counted.* The very section which the Governor quotes as his authority for throwing out the votes of Brazos county, proves that in doing it he perpetrated a base fraud, and violated the plain letter of the law.

But he gives another reason for throwing out the vote of this county, "further, forty-nine persons of foreign birth bad been permitted to register and vote, without legal proof of naturalization." If this be true it proves that he has placed officers as registrars, and Judges of election, who are either too ignorant to understand their duty, or too fraudulent and vile to do it.

But if this were true it by no means follows, that the entire vote of the county should be rejected.

Can an illegal vote change the virtue of a legal vote, and make it vicious, because it happens to be placed in the same box? The Governor had just as well throw the vote out in the entire

4th congressional district, because there were forty-nine illegal votes cast in Brazos county in the 3rd district.

The Governor throws out in Freestone county, Fourteen hundred and forty seven votes cast for D. C. Giddings, this he did on the grounds of intimidation, acts of violence and armed disturbance, which he says, had been shown to have materially interfered with the purity and the freedom of the election, thereby preventing such a number of qualified electors therein from voting as would have changed the result of the election in that county if they had been permitted freely to vote." The Governor well knew that no such facts existed in Freestone county, and in order to give semblance of honesty to what he found it necessary to do in order to give Wm. T. Clark the certificate of election he declared martial-law in this county, and threw out the vote. This we firmly believe from the facts, as we know them to exist, and as we believe that he knew them to exist. He had been canvassing that county for Clark, and had surveyed the ground well, and knew that the majority on a fair and full election, in that and Limestone county, would be overwhelming for D. C. Giddings.

The Governor in his statement puts down the vote of Harris county for W. T. Clark, two thousand and thirty-three votes for D. C. Giddings, one thousand six hundred and twenty-one.

The governor does not write opposite of these figures, rejected oh no! but says "six hundred and twenty one voters reported as having been deterred from voting for W. T. Clark, as desired by them, not counted, though those names appear on registration list and though it is likely that some or all of them desired to vote as alleged &c." The Governor says that these men were deterred from voting, and gives as the evidence of this fact, that their names were on the registration list, and because 621 names were found on the registration who did not vote, therefore they were deterred from voting. How monstrous! If the voters themselves did not so state, and he says they did not, how was it known for whom they would vote?

Again, how were they deterred? If by riot, tumult, acts of violence, intimidation, armed disturbance, bribery or corrupt influence, the Governor, to be consistent, would have to throw out the entire vote, for such he did in all those counties in which D. C. Giddings had a majority. He here plainly shows the cloven foot. In Limestone the vote stood Clark, twenty-eight; Giddings, one thousand, one hundred and fifty-three—all rejected by the Governor. We have fully shown that martial law was the trick gotten up by the Governor and his officials, to throw out this vote. Washington county gave Clark two thousand, five hundred and thirty-five votes, and gave Giddings two thousand, three hundred and sixty eight. The Governor in his statement, puts down and counts for Clark the full two thousand, five hundred and thirty-five votes, and rejects all the votes cast for D. C. Giddings, except one hundred and ten, and gives as his reason for doing so: "the votes received at the 'white man's' place of voting, at what was called the 'white man's ballot boxes,' are rejected, because two voting places are not allowed by law." Where did the Governor get this law from? May not two boxes be at the same voting place? He does not say that these two boxes were at two places, nor were they at two places, but both were at the same voting place, one in one window of the room where the election was held and the other in the other window; this arrangement was made by the judges of election, to facilitate voting. Two boxes at the same voting place, is a very different thing from "two voting places." Section 6, of the election law, declares "All elections for State, District and county officers, shall be held at the county seats of the several counties, and the polls shall be open for four days, from eight o'clock, A. M., until five o'clock, P. M., of each day, with an hour's recess from 12 M. to 1 o'clock, P. M." This section does not prohibit the use of two boxes, nor can the Governor conclude, because two boxes were used, that therefore the voting was carried on at two places. If the election was held at the county seat of Washington county, it complied with the requirements of the statute, as to the place of holding elections.

But was there not an absolute necessity for more than one box, in order that all the electors should have time to vote? There were four thousand, nine hundred and three (4,903) votes cast in Washington county, and there was only thirty-two hours (32) to cast them in, provided not an hour was lost. This makes eighteen hundred and twenty minutes. Two votes, on an average, are as many as can possibly be deposited a minute. If two a minute voted, only thirty-six hundred and forty, of the four thousand, nine hundred and three, (4,903,) would have been able to vote, leaving thirteen hundred and three (1,303) electors who could not vote for want of time. Would this not have prevented, in the language of the law, "a fair, free, full vote of all the qualified electors of said county?" To show that not more than two votes can be deposited in a minute, we need only point out what the law requires the voters and judges of election to do:

By Section 13, the judge of election "shall have power to administer oaths and affirmations to persons offering to vote at any election conducted by them, and to examine such person, under oath, touching their right to vote at such election." It will take at least five minutes to administer the oath, ask the questions and receive the answers of the applicant.

One of the judges of election keeps the record of registry of names, another receives the votes. The judge who keeps the record is to look through the record and find the name of each person offering to vote, and call out his name aloud, and mark opposite his name, on the registration list, the letter V. By Section 19, where a voter has not the right to vote for all the officers to be elected, the judge of the election is to write one or all the words "State," "District," and "Congress," according as the voter of such ticket shall have the right to vote for State or District officers and members of Congress, or a portion of the same. All this takes time.

By Section 17th, the judge of election may *require* any person offering to vote "to make oath and declare, he is the person to whom was issued the registration certificate, or other paper upon which he offers to vote, and that he has not voted at any other poll or voting place." This will take in each case five minutes. This plainly shows that it was the sworn duty of the Governor, under the laws and under the injunction of the Constitution, requiring him to take care that the laws of the State be faithfully executed, to have himself provided the means which would have enabled every elector of Washington county, to have voted with ease and convenience at the election. This could only be done by having two boxes opened at the same time and place. It is not true, as the Governor intimates in his reason for rejecting the votes cast for D. C. Giddings, in Washington county, that the votes were cast at two different voting places, and if it be true that the "white man's box" was not presided over by even one lawful officer, it is his fault and not the fault of the people. The fact, if it be a fact, that the box was called the white man's box, had nothing to do with the legality or illegality of the votes which it contained, and his Excellency is welcome to all the capital he can make out of such slang. Doubtless the freedmen did call that the "white man's box," so they called all the tickets which were printed on white paper "the white man's tickets," and all the blue or green "the freedman's tickets." If such slang is a ground for throwing out tickets, every ticket in the State would have been thrown out.

But the Governor gives another reason for throwing out the votes for D. C. Giddings. "Also because four hundred and fifty eight aliens were registered on declaration of intention of becoming citizens, made by them in vacation, before a clerk, and not in term time, before a competent court, of whom all or nearly all, voted at what was called the white man's box,' and for other sufficient causes." And, from this count determine whether the Governor neglected the four hundred and fifty-eight, because they were cast by persons improperly registered, on declaration of intention to become citizens, because the declaration was made in vacation, before a clerk, or because all or nearly all, "voted at what was called the 'white man's Box.' If the former, it matters not what box they were placed in, if that made them illegal they ought not to have been counted, even, had they been deposited in what was called, "the Black man's box." But what does the law say upon this subject of foreigners or aliens making declaration of intention before clerks? Act of Congress of the United States, approved 26th May, A. D. 1824, section two reads: "No certificates of citizenship or naturalization heretofore obtained from any court of record within the United States, shall be deemed invalid in consequence of an omission to comply with the requisition of the first section of the act entitled "an act relative to evidence in cases of naturalization, passed the 22nd day of March one thousand eight hundred and sixteen.

Section third (3rd) of the same act, entitled "*an act in further addition to* "an act to establish an uniform rule of naturalization and to repeal the acts heretofore passed on that subject."

"The declaration required by the first condition specified in the first section of the act to which this is an addition, shall if the same has been *bona fide* made before the *clerk* of either of the courts in the said condition named, be as valid as if it had been made before the *said courts* respectively." This act "*seems to require that*" the Governor should not have thrown these votes out, because the declaration of becoming a citizen was made before a clerk, and not "before a competent court." It would have been much better for the Governor had he never given any reason for throwing the votes for Giddings out. For his reasons condemn him, whether you apply them to the facts or to the law. I will now inform the Governor that in Grimes county there were two boxes run during the whole election, on every day of the election, and the boxes were not even in the same room of the courthouse, and one of the boxes was called "the white man's box" too; not only so the Registrar appointed by the Governor for Grimes county, Mr. R. N. Mills who managed the box at which the freedmen voted, would not let a white man vote at that box, or stand about it. Mr. Mangrum and Mr. Black superintended "the white man's box," and no negroes were allowed by them to vote at that box. Why did not the Governor throw out this vote, the answer is evident, Grimes gave Clark as returned, one thousand six hundred and ninety eight votes, and D. C. Giddings only one thousand two hundred and ninety three. Now if the votes cast in Washington county were illegal because they were put in the box called "the white man's box," would the votes cast in Grimes county by the same purity of reasoning, not be illegal, which were placed in the box called "the negroe's box," or is that the "*one place* provided by law?"

The certificate of election which the Governor gave W. T. Clark, instead of being *prima facie* evidence of his election, and right to the seat in Congress, contains within itself the proof that D. C. Giddings was duly elected to Congress by a majority of the votes of the qualified electors of the third congressional district of the State of Texas. Governor Davis is the lion of this house of corruption, when he comes forth, shakes his manes, and roars, his voice is heard from one end of the State to the other, and his officials tremble at the sound thereof, and stand ready to do any thing he may command.

"Why man, he doth bestride the narrow world,
Like a Collossus, and we petty men
Walk under his large legs, and peep about
To find ourselves dishonorable graves.
Men at some time, are masters of thei r fates :
The fault, dear Brutus, is not in our stars
But in ourselves that we are underlings
Now in the names of all the gods at once,
Upon what meat doth this our Caesar feed
That he is grown so great? Age, thou art shamed,
Rome, thou hast lost the breed of noble bloods,
When went there by an age, since the great flood,
But it was famed, with more than with one man
When could they say, till now, that talked of Rome,
That her wide walks encompass'd but one man?
Now is it Rome indeed, and room enough,
When there is in it but one only man."

THE END.

www.ingramcontent.com/pod-product-compliance
Lightning Source LLC
LaVergne TN
LVHW021402110826
845150LV00007B/1752